Introduction

We're on the road again. Our first two books, The Cheap Way Round and Still Goin' have both done very well and Waterstones now stock them in almost all of their stores in Scotland. The problem for us is that we have to deliver the books to most of these stores. Although the girls and boys in Waterstones in East Kilbride help out as much as they can.

The first book covered mainly the west and central areas of Scotland, relatively close to our homes. We travelled much further afield in our second book, covering more of Scotland, but not the northern and eastern areas.

We felt we needed to do something really different for this, our third book. We would still use our bus passes and of course check out the bars, and more importantly, the quality of the service. Those are the main elements of our mission statement after all.

The idea of the overall theme for this book came to us one night after a particularly exhausting meeting in our local 'The Lum'. One of us, exactly who it was has never been ascertained, came up with the brilliant idea of going round the whole coast of Scotland. So travelling around the entire coast is what we set out to do, sort of, nearly.

These moments of clear thinking are usually the result of at least six pints of medium to strong ale.

In the course of carrying out this master plan of circumnavigation we encountered three main problems.

The first was a recurring one, we get lost, quite a lot. But this just means we often end up in a different place to the one planned.

The second one was also a recurring. Our ability (well John's) to read timetables is not improving with age. Like the first problem, we again ended up in different places from the ones planned.

The end result of the above two problems didn't bother us, and we're sure you won't be too bothered about it either.

The third problem only came to light when we had finished quite a few of our journeys. At one meeting, again held in 'the Lum', we were trying to guage how many more journeys we would need to complete the final stages of our attempt to travel round the coast of Scotland. It turned out to be a depressingly large number.

We came to the conclusion that if we put all of those journeys into one book most of our elderly readers would be struggling to lift the bloody thing. So we made an executive decision to miss out that afore mentioned top bit.

It was decided that since we had already announced that we would be producing a trilogy of books based on our adventures it might be a good idea to make it a four part trilogy. This might seem a little bit odd but, as has been implied above there was a certain amount of alcohol involved in our decision making processes.

The fourth, and hopefully final, part of the trilogy will cover the far North and the Inner Hebrides

'Goin' Roon the Edge' starts in Berwick-on-Tweed, which is in England, and finishes in Dumfries, which isn't. In the following thirteen chapters we will describe the journeys we undertook to travel round our coast.

The journeys were completed in what can only be described as a random fashion as we found it impractical to follow a linear path around the country.

Goin' Roon the Edge

This book is again dedicated
to the two women who
put up with us and make sure
we are properly put out
(also the staff of Waterstones EK)

Goin' Roon the Edge

Craig Stevenson and John Mackay

CONTENTS;

Introduction   7

1.   We came, we saw, we missed the bus   12

2.   The lost city of Portpatrick   34

3.   It's no a bin yer in   50

4.   Big journey to Wee Toon   68

5.   Well away in Galloway   86

6.   No Smokies ban in Arbroath   102

7.   To the Kingdom we come   122

8.   No lock in at the 'Lock Inn'   140

9.   A Fairlie nice day oot   162

10.   The two old Chappies o' Lower Largo   180

11.   Par for the Course   198

12.   Billeted in Banff   216

13.   Doin' time in Peterhead   236

In fact the last two trips saw us abandon our tried and tested day trip format in favour of an overnight stay up in the north east.

Although this appears to suggest that we have given up our cheap way round principles we did manage to travel over four hundred miles by bus for free.

We are again using the Russell Standard. For any reader who has not read our last book, Still Goin', the standard is based on our local barman Russell, who claims to be the world's best barman, and as our wives agree, that's pretty much a done deal. The way it works is as follows, bar staff in the pubs we visit are compared to our chosen benchmark, Russell, and awarded points up to the top standard of five Russells R R R R R. This places them on a par with the great man himself. There is a sliding scale down to R which signifys a level of service which should alert the would be traveller that he or she should avoid this pub like the plague.

We hope that our little adventures will inspire other bus pass holders around the country to get out and about on the occasional free day out. It might be an idea to do this quite soon, before the politicians decide that free bus passes are no longer a vote winner and do away with them for good.

If you do manage to follow in our footsteps there is one thing you should remember, alcohol is not essential for the enjoyment of a good day out. We have been assured, by people who claim to know about such things, that a good cup of tea and the occasional half coated digestive biscuit is every bit as good as a bit of a bevy.

For our part we believe that a few pints, drank sensibly, helps the day along just fine.

Goin' Roon the Edge

Goin' Roon the Edge
2012

Book three sees us travel around the edge of this great country, or as much of it as we could manage in the allotted time.

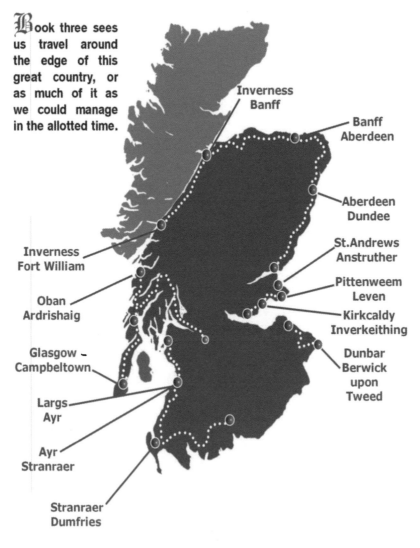

Inverness
Banff

Banff
Aberdeen

Aberdeen
Dundee

St.Andrews
Anstruther

Pittenweem
Leven

Kirkcaldy
Inverkeithing

Dunbar
Berwick
upon
Tweed

Inverness
Fort William

Oban
Ardrishaig

Glasgow
Campbeltown

Largs
Ayr

Ayr
Stranraer

Stranraer
Dumfries

We came, we saw, we missed the bus

*(Across the border we boldly invaded
But to stay a while we were not persuaded)*

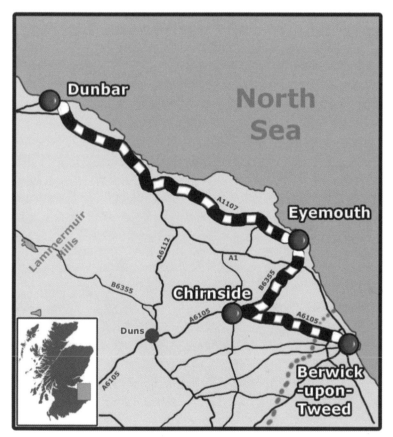

*Berwick-on-Tweed-Chirnside-Eyemouth
Dunbar-Edinburgh*

Goin' Roon the Edge

John; While we waited and hoped that our second book, 'Still Goin' would be taken up by some publisher or 'Waterstones', we were keen to start work on our third book which we both decided would catalogue our travels round the edge of Scotland using our bus passes, or, as happened on this, our first trip, as near the edge as my ability to read a timetable would allow. You would think that by now I'd know how to organize a trip without making a complete arse of it.

The funny thing is that it was a complicated and long trip to plan and complete in one day and I was pleased that I'd managed it. It meant leaving the house at about six in the morning and not getting home until about eleven at night-with long periods of no bevy-what we'll do for our art!

The plan was to start at Berwick-upon-Tweed, then go to Eyemouth, Dunbar and North Berwick and Edinburgh before getting the bus back to Glasgow.

I was a bit worried that Craig, who can be a slow starter in the morning, would not fancy the early start, but he was up for it. Another problem I encountered when checking the timetable, was that the bus from Edinburgh to Berwick-upon-Tweed, which is in England, was in fact the London bus and we could not use our bus passes, this meant paying about £13 each for a single, and that is with our oldies discount. As I could not think of a way round it without missing out on the English part of the trip, we paid the money.

I would not have minded missing out on Berwick-upon-Tweed, but Craig was determined to start in the enemy's territory and slag them off.

Craig; *We decided that this first journey in our latest birl around Scotland really had to be something special. Invading England seemed to fit the bill perfectly.*

I really had to argue my case with John to have Berwick-upon-Tweed included in our itinerary. Since we were setting out to

13

travel around the edge of the country, and Berwick upon Tweed not being in Scotland, he perhaps had reason to argue.

Just to make life interesting, I left the planning of the trip in John's capable hands. Only time would tell just how capable those hands actually were.

In the initial stages of planning he produced one of his legendary spread sheet timetables. On it he had only allowed a few minutes between us getting off the bus from Glasgow and getting onto the National Express bus down to Berwick. There were two huge problems with this idea.

The biggest of these was of course the very tight timetabling of this change over. Even in ordinary times we could easily have been late getting into Edinburgh Bus Station. One wee traffic jam and the gemme would very definitely be a bogey. The fact that Edinburgh City Council have, in their infinite wisdom, decided to dig up most of the main streets to lay tram lines meant we could never be sure when we would arrive at the bus station.

Just from looking at how well they are proceeding with this suggests to us that the trams will be obsolete long before the track is all down. Maybe when they finally get all the track down, they could drive the trams straight to the transport museum.

The other problem we faced was the troubling fact that we had to pay for the trip down to Berwick; full fare. If we missed our connection in Edinburgh we wouldn't only be scuppered for this entire trip but, more importantly, we would be £27.00 out of pocket. With that in mind we decided to start out on the trip quite a bit earlier than the spread sheet magician had originally planned.

John; It was a lovely, but chilly start to the trip. I had remembered that there was an early morning bus from East Kilbride to Edinburgh, so even though it meant leaving half an hour earlier than if we were going via Glasgow, we saved

14

about an hour and a half in travelling time. The journey took us through Hamilton, Motherwell, New Stevenston, Holytown and other wee places before hitting the M8 and then it was no time before we were in our capital city of Edinburgh, or as we call it, the city with no trams.

While we're talking about the crazies who run the country, or in this case, Edinburgh, we stood and watched dozens of workmen not working at digging up one of the streets off Princess Street. Not only that, but the council are paying commercial artists to produce paintings of what the street they are digging up will look like with the trams running! Surely it's daft enough to continue throwing money literally down a hole in the road without paying artists to produce drawings of something that is going to happen so far in the future, if at all. The drawings themselves will be old masters by the time the trams start running. However, the artists' impressions were very nice.

We still had a bit of time to kill so we found a wee back street café called 'Snax Cafe' which was great and very reasonable. We would recommend it to anyone looking for a great breakfast in Edinburgh that you can afford.

Edinburgh was freezing so we wasted no time in getting to the bus station and after getting a paper, water and a Bounty Bar (with three pieces) we got on our bus, the City Link 904, to Berwick-upon-Tweed in England.

Craig; I don't usually like early starts. The thing is I rarely go to bed until the wee small hours. This sometimes leads people to believe that I'm not a morning person. But as far as I'm concerned five o'clock is still the middle of the night.

As it was, I didn't get a wink of sleep the night before our trip. So it is quite understandable that I wasn't at my best when John arrived at my door, his usual cheery self, at six. It turned out that my sleepless night was a bit of a blessing in disguise.

15

Goin' Roon the Edge

I had insisted that we book our seats on the East Kilbride to Edinburgh bus. Just in case it was very busy. In fact I even convinced John that we should get on the bus at the stop before the town centre. Once again, just in case.

This bus is essentially for office workers and students who are trying to save a bob or two, so I had every expectation of a very busy bus. There were four passengers on board! I hadn't taken into account the down turn in the economy and the reluctance of students to get out of bed before mid-day.

The bus stopped to take on a few more passengers in each of the towns we passed through. At least I think it did. I was fast asleep for most of the journey. It was great.

Most of our fellow travellers got off at the bus stop before the bus station. I was surprised at how many people there were on board. In fact I half wondered if they were getting on again at the back of the bus.

Round at the station we checked the departure board then went for a stroll to kill some time until our next bus was due to leave. We had about an hour and a half to wait and so it seemed like a good idea to find somewhere to get a bite to eat.

The wee back street café we found was magic, though I have to admit that it didn't look like much to start with. Any description of a place which starts with the phrase 'back street' doesn't usually end well.

It was only because John insisted that we went in at all. I'm glad he did as the food was good and the price was very reasonable.

After we had finished our rolls on sausage and cups of tea John suggested a little sightseeing. This just didn't sound like John at all. It took me a good five minutes before I realised what he was up to. What he was actually up to was scouring the neighbourhood for early opening pubs. Legend has it that some city centre pubs open before 10.00am. I think it was more wishful thinking than legend, personally, but the man is obsessed.

Actually what he was, was unlucky. But it was really just as well his luck was not in as it turned out that although our big National Express coach did have a toilet on board it was out of order.

John would have been in great danger on the long journey down to Berwick-on-Tweed with a couple of pints of his favourite brackish water swilling around in his bladder. With no working toilet on board he would have been in agony. Come to think of it so would I as I would have to listen to him whining, mile after mile.

John hopes to avoid fallen arches.

John; After our Geordie driver had done his comedy routine of telling us all about the bus and the rules, basically that there was no enjoying yourselves, he told us the Toilet was out of order. I had just taken a huge drink of water and nearly choked at the thought of an hour and a half without being able to go.

17

You know what it's like, if there is a toilet, you don't need to go-you know the rest. He said it was going to be fixed at some service station halfway down England!

Luckily, my bladder was to the fore and we had a nice run down the East of Scotland. I have never been down this way before. It is nice, but a lot flatter and less dramatic than the West. There are a lot of fields that are bright yellow. It is a bit sore on the eyes, especially if you have a wee bit of a hangover, which I had. Craig told me it was rape seed, or something like that.

Craig was mad that there was no sign on the road saying we were entering England, so he had nothing to spit at. He also claimed that the atmosphere changed when we went into England. I think he's off his head.

Our bus arrived right on time, 11.05am and we started wandering up the main street to find out where our next bus left from before we got into the bevy. We had no luck finding where the bus left for Eyemouth, but we did notice that the first three pubs we passed were all closed. This was a worry.

Things got so bad trying to find a pub that was open that we ended up going into a Wetherspoon's, because it was open. Now I've nothing against these pubs, they are comfortable and the drink is very cheap (compared to other pubs), but they don't feel like a real pub, and there are always weans running about. I don't like that. Even worse for Craig was that there were paper flyers on all the tables telling him it was St. George's Week and special meals were being offered. Steam was coming out of his ears.

While we were trying to enjoy our first pint of the day in England, I asked a wee man where our next bus left from. We had found out that it left from Chapel Street, but had no idea where it was. The wee man was very nice and friendly and after telling us the directions, came racing back five minutes later to tell us that he had given us the wrong directions and wanted to make sure we had the right directions in case we came back looking for him. What a man!

As we wanted to find a real pub, and the wee man had told us that there was a good pub opposite where the bus left from, we decided to wander up there, see a bit of the town, and have another pint.

Craig; I was spared a lot of unnecessary sightseeing as I managed to nod off again just a couple of miles into our journey. Just before we crossed the border I managed to waken up. We had wanted to get a photo of the sign right on the border but we were out of luck. There wasn't one. Not one we could see anyway. These scrap thieves are getting outrageous!

Berwick-on-Tweed has seen an awful lot of history. It has belonged to both England and Scotland many times over the centuries. In fact as recently as a couple of years ago more than 60% of its citizens, questioned in an opinion poll run by a national newspaper, said they wanted Berwick to become part of Scotland again. Although I think that might have more to do with free prescriptions and care for the elderly than a love of stovies and bagpipe music.

If their change of nationality is ever to come about there are a couple of things they are going to have to sort out. Most importantly they will have to take a look at their licencing laws.

All pubs should be opened by 11.00am, at the latest! There is just no excuse for opening your pubs after mid-day. Do these people not know that there are bus travellers out there who have journeyed many miles to visit their annoying little town?

We had both been quite excited as our bus drove through the town. From our high vantage point we could see quite a few nice looking pubs. It was only after we got off the bus we realised that all the great pubs we had just seen were shut. This, as you can imagine, did not go down well with us.

After a fruitless twenty minute wander around the back streets we ended up in a pub which was directly across the road from where the bus had let us off. Unfortunately it was one of those brewer's chain pubs which we are not too keen on, they tend to attract the Jakie element of society with their rock bottom prices.

Happily this pub, a 'Wetherspoons', no point in naming it as they're all the same, was completely Jakie free. It was however 'hoaching' with weans. I'm not that keen on the noise the wee deranged buggers make at the best of times but, at half past eleven on a Monday morning, and in a foreign country at that, they were driving me nuts.

Barman Rating ℞℞℞,

John fancied a wee bucket in the barrels.

Goin' Roon the Edge

John had asked for directions to our next bus stop at the bar and one of the customers had been very helpful.
Twenty minutes later John was wishing he had never asked.

John; It was at this time I had a bad feeling about my timetable reading ability. When we were almost at the bus stop, a number 253 passed going to Eyemouth. I had a note that it was a number 235 we were getting. Worse still, when we checked the timetable at the stop, we found out that the next bus to Eyemouth was leaving at 1.55, not 12.30 as I had confidently predicted. As we were working to a tight schedule, and our first impressions of Berwick and its pubs were pretty grim, Craig started lambasting me about this screw up. Worse was to follow when I suggested going in to the pub across the road, '*The Cobbled Yard Hotel*'. The only plus thing you could say about it was that it was open. We had a look around and straight back out.

We decided to go for a wander and try and find a decent pub and decide what to do. If we waited for the bus at 1.55, we would have to change where we were going. This was a nightmare. A clear head and a pint were needed.

After wandering down toward the river and up cobbled streets, which Craig hates because they hurt his feet, what a wimp, we found a pub called '*The Barrels Ale House*' and things started to improve. It was an amazing pub, old fashioned and very hard to describe. One of the chairs at the bar was a dentist's, or barber's chair. The barmaid Jackie, who was great, had no idea. The first impression of the inside was it was a dump, but it wasn't. It was great.

An amazing thing about the pub was that when you went into the gents, it was like a toilet in a nightclub in Soho, all black tiles. All it needed was flashing lights. The bottom of the cubicle door was about two foot off the ground. Just thought I would give you this bit of information.

We explained to Jackie what we were doing and our problems with getting to our next destination, and after a couple of great pints and a great laugh, Jackie came up with the plan of getting a taxi up to the train station and getting the 12.52 number 60 bus which would take us to Chirnside. We would get off there, cross the road and get on the number 37 Alex Wait and Son bus to Eyemouth. This bus left Chirnside at 1.16 which was about five minutes after we arrived. This seemed like a great plan as it meant we would be in Eyemouth at about half past one, just a wee bit later than planned.

Jackie ordered the taxi and it was with great sadness that we left her great pub. One not to miss if you are in Berwick-on-Tweed, probably the only one.

We were only waiting a few minutes when what I thought was our bus arrived, so I got on first and asked for a single to Chirnside. The bus driver was from the North East of England and said he had never heard of Chirnside. I was in the middle of telling him this was a bit unusual for the bus driver not to know where he was going when Craig told me this was a bus for Newcastle. Never mind, you can't embarrass me.

Craig;. It would seem John had made a total arse of our timetable for that day.

After all the nonsense I had to put up with from him after I made a few simple planning mistakes last year, I didn't know whether to quietly seeth with indignation or laugh like a drain at his predicament. I chose the laughing option.

Out of spite for doing this John insisted we needed to go on what turned out to be a pointless forced march along the banks of the River Tweed.

The town of Berwick-on-Tweed is quite picturesque in a market town sort of a way. But the river bank, or at least the bit we saw, was definitely a bit on the manky side.

By sheer chance we found a real pub. The Barrels Ale House, *or the Barrels as the locals call it, was a wonderful wee place; very odd, but wonderful just the same.*

We were complementing the girl on having such a nice old pub as a place of work when she told us that it wasn't all that old. She reckoned it was only about twenty years old and had only been decorated to look as if it had been there forever.

Apparently it came third in a national real ale competition.

To celebrate this great achievement I ordered a pint of Stella. The young barmaid was very helpful, but I don't really think she understood what we were trying to do with our travels.

John came up with what he thought was a great idea. He suggested that we could make up some of the time we had lost by getting the train to Eyemouth. Unfortunately the barmaid shot down his master plan immediately by informing us that Eyemouth didn't have a railway station. John was crushed. I chose the laughing option, again.

Barmaid Rating; 🍺🍺🍺🍺🍺

It was at this point I had my own little brainwave. Using my super-duper all singing all dancing smartphone, I found a way to get to our next destination, eventually.

The only problem was that we needed to get a bus from Berwick railway station in the next twenty minutes. We had no way of managing it on foot. The barmaid said she had a friend who had a taxi and could get us there on time.

Her friend turned out to be a very friendly lady who gave us a potted history of Berwick's recent past as we hurtled along back streets to the station.

She told us about the council knocking down historical buildings for developers to put up modern private housing, and about the closure of some of the town's best pubs.

I told her about my idea to get a bus to a place called Chirnside where we would catch another bus which would take us to Eyemouth. She said that it sounded crazy and as soon as I had finished telling her about it, so did I.

While we were on the subject of crazy ideas I asked her why the buses all left from the railway station. I really should have known the answer. They had knocked the bus station down to build more new houses.

John; Our bus arrived, a worrying five minutes late and we were delighted to find out that we could use our bus pass, because we were going into Scotland. This cheered us up no end.

It was a nice wee run to Chirnside, but it looked as if we might be a wee bit tight to get the next bus, and with my luck today, I feared the worst. I had a word with the driver as we came into Chirnside to suggest he drop us off right away, but he assured me that he would take us right to the square where the next bus would be waiting. As we stopped in the square, our next bus was parked across the road, and as we got off our bus it buggered off without us. Our driver tried to get the other bus's attention by honking his horn, but to no avail. I think I said for goodness sake, or something like that, as the bus disappeared down the road without us.

I was in a complete panic. This was a very small village and I knew that the next bus might be hours, if there was one. Craig just said it was all my fault. He was just getting revenge for all the slagging I give him for his screw ups.

There was a pub across the road called *'The Red Lion',* it looked shut, but it wasn't, so we went in.

The old saying that 'It's darkest before the dawn' was never used better than today. It was another great pub with a great landlady called Maureen and a great local called John with his wee dog called Jockey, which he took everywhere.

John said he bought Jockey when he won over £500,000 on the pools. I thought I should get to know this bloke until he told us

John tries to get wee Jocky's autograph.

that there were 16 of them that won the money about 10 years ago. Ah well, he was still a nice bloke.

We had a great time in the pub, and even Craig, who wanted to slag me about another screw up was enjoying himself. It got even better when, after explaining what we were doing and showing our first book, John bought it. What a guy!

The pints were going down well and Maureen spent ages with timetables planning the rest of our trip. At this stage I was just happy to be there.

The plan she came up was that we would get the 3.07 to Eyemouth, then a bus an hour later to Dunbar, and miss out

North Berwick altogether as she said it is full of snobs and golfers and not worth the bother. I'm sure it's not as bad as that but we decided to follow her plan, as mine had gone down the tube hours ago.

She also said she would have a word with the driver who buggered off without us. She said it would be the same driver on our 3.07 bus. The driver's name was Veronica and she was a big, blonde woman. On hearing her description, I reckoned we should be thanking her for allowing us to have a great time in Chirnside. I'm also a shitbag.

A very interesting fact about Chirnside is that it is where the greatest racing driver of all time, Jim Clark lived almost all his life and is buried. John, the local, was a friend of Jim and told us all about him. There is a monument and a plaque in the square about Jim. I took a photo of it.

John told us that the pub normally shuts in the afternoon and we thanked Maureen very much for keeping it open just for us. I am starting to think that East of Scotland people are magic.

We said our goodbyes to Maureen, John and Jocky and got the 3.07 bus to Eyemouth. Veronica, the driver who left us standing earlier was really funny and we had a great laugh all the way to Eyemouth. We never mentioned her leaving us earlier, for obvious reasons.

Chirnside, by the way, is a lovely wee town and well worth a visit if only to pay homage to the great Jim Clark and visit a magic wee pub.

Craig; The bus we were looking for was going to Galashiels via Chirnside. Quite why John would jump aboard the Newcastle bus was a bit of a mystery to me. It rather mystified the driver too as he had never heard of Chirnside. That made three of us. After dragging John off the wrong bus and on to the right one we settled down for the fifteen minute trip. The fact that it took twenty minutes was a bit of a worry.

Goin' Roon the Edge

We were meant to be connecting with our next bus somewhere in the middle of Chirnside. But since we knew hee-haw about Chirnside it was hard to know where the middle was. We just had to depend on our driver. That was, on reflection, a bit of a mistake.

Granted he did try to stop the other bus, but if he had just let us off a stop earlier we would have caught our next bus quite easily.

Then again if we had managed this manoeuvre we would have missed out on a great pub visit. The Red Lion was very much the traditional village pub. It was a wee bit old fashioned, exactly the way we like our pubs to be.

I had never heard of Chirnside before, and said so. The barmaid, who was also the owner, and her only other customer seemed shocked to hear this.

The customer, an older gentleman, gave me a short history of his little town and I found myself apologising for my thickness. I now know, as I should have anyway, that Chirnside was the home town of the late great Jim Clark, world champion racing driver.

My new history teacher, John Kinghorn, was really interesting to talk to. The fact that he bought one of our books in no way influenced this last comment.

John Kinghorn was a friend of the Clark family and had some very nice and interesting things to tell us about the formula one champion. It was a privilege to listen to him talk about what Jim Clark was like when he wasn't rubbing shoulders with the famous people of his day. His stories painted a picture of a quiet, down to earth and pleasant man.

Apparently the people of the town and surrounding area paid to have a monument raised to Clark's memory. Stupidly I asked where we could see the structure.

Maureen, the barmaid, and John didn't so much as snigger when it was pointed out to me that I had been standing next to it when I got off the bus. Indeed I had been looking at it ever since we had come into the pub. Every time I looked out of the window to check the time on the large town clock I was looking directly at it.

Maureen ensured herself a five star write up when she produced a set of bus timetables and re-planned the rest of our route for us.

Barmaid Rating ℞℞℞℞℞

John; The bus, which was actually a minivan with seats, dropped us off outside *'The Tavern',* which is situated on the front in Eyemouth.

The design of the pub is not very nice, all sort of modern and flat sides, but inside it is very nice with a dance floor and cosy bar. The girl behind the bar was very nice and helpful and when I asked her if she knew a guy I worked with for years who had moved to Eyemouth, she not only knew him, but his dog's names as well. I love these wee places where everyone knows everyone else.

The bar had a great view over the sea to Norway or somewhere Scandinavian. I left my details with the barmaid and asked her to give them to Big John (that's his name) next time he was in. Because of the rush we were now in because of earlier timetable irregularities, or my screw-ups if you believe Craig, I had no time to try to find Big John.

As we left the pub for the 50 yard walk up the hill to the stop, a bus passed us going up the hill. You should have heard what Craig said. I knew we were due a break with the buses today and was rewarded when our bus, the 235 that I had originally planned for us to be on turned up on time.

The journey to Dunbar takes the best part of an hour because it detours through every village on the way. I like this as you see some really nice places. Craig slept most of the way as he did on all our buses today. He claimed he got no sleep last night because he had to get up at five this morning and he hadn't got to his bed until Two. Maybe that's why he was in a bad mood and blaming me for all the screw ups today, or maybe it was because of all my screw ups today!

Craig; On the wee bus to Eyemouth our driver Veronica chatted away to us. We were her only passengers. She was such a good laugh we decided not to bring up the subject of bus drivers leaving people stranded in the middle of nowhere. It was her who had been driving that earlier bus. But things had worked out well so we didn't do any of the nasty things we said we'd like to do when we caught up with the 'bad person' who had left us there.

Since we only had about three quarters of an hour to spend in Eyemouth, she told us that our best bet would be to settle for a drink in The Tavern. As it was only a few yards from the bus stop we agreed that it was a great idea.

From the outside The Tavern didn't look up to much. It was no surprise to find that this theme continued on the inside as well. There was a definite feeling of the community centre about the place. However, it was very clean and the young barmaid was quite chatty.

Because we had so little time to spare we decided to limit our intake of booze. There is no point in rushing your drink. I managed a manly pint and a half of lager while John wimped out by only having a pint of his favourite coloured water and a wee hauf of vodka.

Barmaid Rating 🍺🍺🍺🍺

Even then we were a bit late getting to the bus stop. On the way to it a bus shot past us and John nearly had a seizure. I was in two minds whether to leave him behind, or heroically carry him on to the bus stop. Since he was holding the kitty I decided that if he keeled over I would be obliged to help him.

John; Dunbar is a much bigger place than Eyemouth and there seemed to be a few pubs about. I was praying some of them would be open. We got off the bus and wandered down to the

29

harbour and stoated about taking a few photos of the fishing boats. The harbour itself was a bit wasted by a lot of the properties looking very modern in design and out of place in this ancient setting. How about that for fancy words?

The first pub we visited was called *'The Castle Hotel'*. There were a few people in and the atmosphere was good. The barman was helpful but we didn't have a chance to speak to him much as Craig needed a seat as his cobbled streets affected feet were killing him. It was a pleasant place and the beer was good. One problem was that because of the relatively few pints we had drunk and the time spent on buses, we were still sober, and this was about four in the afternoon. An unusual trip this.

We said goodbye to the barman and wandered along the main street and into our second pub there called *'The Eagle Inn'*. This was another nice pub inside with a good atmosphere. We stood at the bar (Craig's feet had recovered) and had a wee chat with the barmaid, who, by the way she acted, am sure was the owner. She was pleasant enough in a slightly stuck up manner, and like *'The Castle Hotel'*. I would recommend it to any travellers. I think we may have had a couple of pints because when we checked our watches found that it was nearly time for our bus. Craig and I were both hungry, so Craig suggested that as his feet were suddenly hurting again, I should run back to a chip shop we passed and get a couple of fish suppers to eat before we got the bus. You're not allowed to eat hot food on buses, (law number 374 about not enjoying yourselves on buses). So we stood at the stop and enjoyed our fish suppers, which were delicious.

As we had to miss out North Berwick, the next bus, the number X45, was to take us to Edinburgh Bus Station, or that was the plan. But with my luck today, and the fact that the bus said something else on the front, I'm not sure what, I was a wee bit concerned. Sure enough, when we came into the centre of Edinburgh, the bus shot past where the bus station was, going to god knows where. I jumped up and asked the driver where he was going. No idea what he said, the long and short of it was we had to get off the bus and walk back to the bus station, and every back street we went along had cobbles. I was enjoying this.

Craig; The trip to Dunbar didn't take very long and this meant we had a reasonable amount of time exploring the town.

We had seen from the bus that there were quite a few good looking pubs to be visited. Unfortunately John was feeling a bit touristy and demanded that we spend some time sightseeing. I felt I had to agree. Actually I was feeling slightly guilty since the only scenery we had time to appreciate in Eyemouth had been the vista we had clocked from the bar of The Tavern. And to be quite frank, it was a bit manky looking.

Dunbar harbour was quite an interesting place to visit. It is a working harbour, as opposed to the fancy marinas we usually find, so we liked it.

To reward ourselves for all this effort we strolled into The Castle Hotel bar. It was quite an old fashioned bar, but very comfortable.

To be honest, after all that hiking over rough cobbles which I had been forced into, anywhere with seats would have qualified as comfortable. Earlier on I had noticed a pub along the road called The Eagle Inn. Back in my old home town, Auchinleck, I had spent my formative years in a pub of the same name.

This one was different. It was considerably more up market, although, to be honest that's not saying too much.

Back in the early 70s my Eagle was more like a saloon in a frontier town than a trendy bar like this one in Dunbar.

It was a nice enough place and if there had been enough time it could well have been a two pint stop. We did however have enough time to stop at the chippy.

Barman Rating 🍺🍺🍺,

John; After a toilet visit we got on our Number 900 bus back to Glasgow. Craig slept all the way.

By the time we got off the bus in Buchanan Street Bus Station, Craig had had the equivalent of about eight hours sleep and wakened feeling refreshed and looking forward to a visit to *'The Horseshoe'*, our local in Glasgow. We had a couple of pints there before heading over to the Central Station and onto the 10.48pm train to East Kilbride. I must have been reasonably sober to remember that detail.

As usual, Craig's Irene had followed our journey by text. I think she's frightened Craig will run away, which is impossible with his feet. Anyway, I better not slag her off too much as she stayed up late and came and picked us up at the station. The truth of the matter is that she had text'd Craig so much that his high tech phone ran out of battery and she had to phone me to organize the pick-up. Think I'll have to go ex-directory Only kidding Irene!

I arrived back home to an empty house. Kate was in Edinburgh with her niece Julie to see the musical 'Chicago' and was staying over in Edinburgh at Julie's house. So Kate was not in to see how sober I was.

That was the end of our first trip round the edge of Scotland using the bus pass. The fact that we couldn't use the bus pass on our first journey to Berwick, and we ended up inland instead of on the edge for one of our stops does not take away from the fact that we are intrepid travellers who have no idea how a timetable works.

I have decided to reintroduce my recollections of what I have spent in the day. There are two reasons for this, one is that someone said that when they read our first book, they were amazed that I still had my liver and would like to see how long it lasts, but the main reason, apart from annoying Craig's Irene, who thinks it's terrible the amount I drink on a trip, and it is, is that I have been asked by the taxman to fill in a self-assessment

Goin' Roon the Edge

form. I have never filled in one in my life, but my son Gregor's partner Michelle says she will help and that it is no problem, but I should keep receipts and claim for everything. Whether getting pissed on a day out counts has still to be seen. Nothing ventured, nothing gained I always say.

So, remembering that it is my spends, and obviously Craig drinks much less than me (for Irene's peace of mind), I have detailed below very roughly what I spent. It is very roughly because the next day I have very little idea of what happened the day before.

John; *Day's Spends;*

Bus Fares;	£13.00 (so we could slag England)
Food;	£5.00 (Fish Supper)
Train;	£0.80 (back to EK)

So apart from the having to pay to get into England, which was Craigs' idea, it is a reasonably cheap day out. But the devil drink takes over.

Drink;   £30.00 (can't make it any less than 10 pints. I know this sounds a lot, but remember it is spread out from 11 in the morning till about 10 at night. That's my excuse anyway.

Total;   **£48.80**

Note to Irene   Craig only had three pints-honest!

The lost city of Portpatrick

(You should go doon to Stranraer if you're able,
Put money in the jukebox 'n dance on the table)

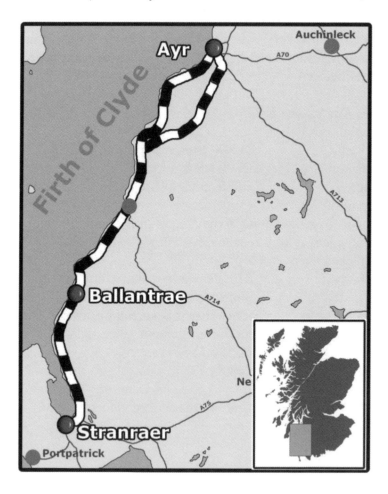

Stranraer-Ballantrae-Ayr

Goin' Roon the Edge

John; This trip was supposed to be from Portpatrick at the very bottom left hand corner of Scotland up to Ayr, stopping at Stranraer and Girvan on the way. At least that's the way I had planned it using our normal web page, 'Traveline Scotland.co.uk'. We have had problems in the past but today was just ridiculous. This web site is great to use, just key in where you're leaving from, where you're going to, the date and time of your travel and it produces, in great detail, all the bus details you need. Now either I'm a complete numpty or Traveline's information is a complete load of keech and out of date-make your own mind up.

Like all of our day trips covering a long distance, it was an early start. I had to be up at 6.30am. The problem I had was that the wife, Kate was away on a trip to Aberdeen with her sister Sheila to visit their pal Sandra, so I had to make my own pieces. This was not the main problem. I hate to admit it but I have no idea how to set the alarm. When you're retired there's no need. Luckily I got Kate to set it before she left the previous morning.

So it was up at 6.30am, make the pieces (corned beef and English mustard as usual) and wander down for Craig.

It was raining heavily and the forecast was crap. Apart from the poor scenic grandeur, the weather does not affect the pubs too much.

Craig; *Portpatrick is pretty close to the edge by anyone's reckoning. It's just not possible to get any further south than that. We thought that old it would make an ideal starting point for one of our trips on our continuing quest to travel along the edge of Scotland.*

I actually spent quite some time planning out this particular journey. To be honest I spent too much time on the early stages of it and not nearly enough on the rest. I blame John for this as I had an awful time trying to persuade him that it was a great wee place to visit. The truth is I don't think he had any idea where it was in the first place.

When I first suggested it as a possible destination he just looked at me with a blank expression. I took this as a sign of apathy, or possible a minor stroke. It was only later that it occurred to me that he was geographically confused. He has never admitted it though. I think he was under the impression that I was suggesting we take a bus run to Ireland, right enough, maybe that could be an idea for book four.

We might have worn out our welcome in too many Scottish pubs by then anyway!

John; Our usual number 18 took us right into Buchanan Street Bus Station where I had to excuse myself and use the facilities in the station. Do you know it's 30p to get in. I was all chuffed when the sign said there was 10p credit in the machine, so I only had to pay 20p and it was worth every penny.

I hate to go on about us oldies and our beloved Parliament, but surely the over 60s should get into the toilets for nothing. It is a well-known fact that we have to go to the toilet on a more regular basis than the younger people with the strong bladders.

Anyway, with a lighter head and a spring in my step I found Craig who had bought some chocolate and got me a Mail. He was holding it by his fingertips in case some of the right wing rantings in the paper affected his left wing Ayrshire mining views.

Craig; Although I've never been to Portpatrick I feel as if I know it well. A couple of years ago Irene and I planned a wee holiday down there so I checked out all the hotels, B & B's and of course pubs in the town via my faithful computer.

It looked really good. The holiday idea had fallen through due to the fact that we didn't fancy a week of dodging from place to place to miss the showers.

Anyway, I had the timetable set for the first and most important part of the journey when John decided he had better do the planning for this one. He thinks I have a bit of a blind spot when it comes to Dumfries and Galloway. He may well be right. My first effort to travel through this wonderful part of Scotland didn't go so well, a fact which I, apparently, will never be able to live down, if John has his way at any rate.

As usual, the day before we were to set off on our latest adventure, I received an e-mail from the great planner himself. Attached was the obligatory spread sheet, detailing our every movement. It looked good, I was just a bit concerned that there was only a five minute gap between arriving in Stranraer and catching our next bus to Portpatrick.

John, however had a contingency plan. If we missed that first bus there was, apparently, enough time to have a quick beer, possibly two, before our next bus out to Portpatrick. What could possibly go wrong? It was foolproof. Let us pause to consider the undisputable fact that nothing, repeat nothing, is foolproof; especially old fool proof.

John; Our bus, the Citylink 923 was a bit late arriving and we were worried because, if possible, we wanted to get the connecting bus from Stranraer to Portpatrick that left about the same time as ours arrived. A worry at the start of the day is terrible, it just plays on your mind the whole trip. The fact that the driver was a wee Irish bloke should have started alarm bells ringing.

When we showed the wee bloke our Bus Passes, he just looked at them as if they were some sort of unknown foreign currency and told us just to get on the bus-magic.

The journey was going fine and the weather was brightening up, although we couldn't see anything because the windows were all steamed up. The problems started when, after leaving Ayr Bus Station, our bus started going along the coast road towards god knows where. We came across road works with diversion signs, and to cut a long mystery tour short, he got lost and ended up asking if there was anyone on the bus who knew where we were. What a laugh, I had already given up on the quick turn round in Stranraer.

This was Craig's chance at being in the limelight. He knew the way back to the main road and gave the wee bloke directions. You'd have thought he'd carried out emergency brain surgery the way he was going on about how great he was. That's the way I remembered it anyway.

Craig; *The day, as they say, started like any other. I got up in the middle of the night and, along with John, caught a bus into Glasgow then hung about waiting for our next bus. The bus station wasn't busy and neither was the queue for the bus to Stranraer. We stood there scanning the horizon for our CityLink bus, wondering if it would be on time.*

The bus that turned up was actually one from the Ulster Bus Company. This didn't really worry us much, but the wee driver should have set the bells ringing.

He parked the bus at our stance, got out then proceeded to make an arse of himself trying to open the barrier to let on the passengers. It was one of these set ups they use to make you queue in the post office. He couldn't get the catch to release. After taking some advice from another driver he managed to work it out. Little did we know that this was to become a bit of a pattern for our little Irish friend.

I had been looking forward to spending quite a lot of time sleeping on this part of the day's proceedings. It was not to be. We arrived in Ayr bus station more or less on schedule, but trouble was in store for us, big time.

John; Back on the main road the wee Irish bus driver did all he could to get back on the timetable. The problem is that after you leave Ayr, the road to Stranraer is one lane each way for almost all of the journey, and with the number of heavy goods vehicles going up and down on their way to and from Ireland, the road is a nightmare. I would hate to have to drive along it on a regular basis.

Goin' Roon the Edge

By the way, Craig and I and the girls are off to Tenerife this Saturday for a holiday, and while we were enjoying the scenery through the misted up windows, Craig got a text from Irene saying that she had been on to some BBC web page and the temperature in Tenerife when we arrive was going to be 39 degrees. What a woman! We reckoned she was looking at Tel-Aviv or somewhere like that.

The rest of the journey passed without incident and we enjoyed the lovely scenery and passed through some nice looking wee places like Ballantrae, which looked like a nice wee place for a stop. A funny thing is when you look out the window at The Ailsa Craig, or Paddy's Milestone, you never seem to pass it, it is always facing you, amazing.

After dropping off almost all of the passengers at Cairnryan to catch the ferry to Ireland, our driver spent about 10 minutes talking to another bus driver instead of getting us to our destination. The knock on effect of his chat was that as we approached our bus stop, a bus turned in front of us and went up a road that was signposted Portpatrick, I was certain this was our 11.05 bus. We were really brassed off, but still gave the driver a polite thank you as we left the bus. Breeding is everything. It was raining heavily again.

A funny thing about this area is that there are about three different terminals from which Car Ferries can leave for Ireland. They must have cost a fortune to build. You'd think that one would be enough and all the companies could share the costs involved. Or is this too simple?

Craig; *Neither John nor me can actually work out why anyone would want to take a very large coach through the suburbs of Ayr, when there is a fairly serviceable bypass just sitting there. It took us quite a while to realize our wee driver was completely lost. Instead of just admitting this he persevered. The roads got narrower as we got more and more concerned. I might actually have said something, we were sitting only two*

39

seats behind him, but I imagined he was going to a pick-up point. Apart from insanity, what other reason could he have for lumbering through these tiny little streets? He certainly put the wind up a few of the locals who were unfortunate enough to be out driving at that time. I think it was when he drove into that cul-de sac that I began to lose faith in him. In total I think we lost about 15 minutes while 'wee paddy mayhem' made a complete arse of himself navigating us around the suburbs of Ayr.

Something had to be done! When the bus came to a juddering halt at a road closed sign he finally admitted he didn't know where the hell he was. He actually shouted. 'Does anyone know the way out of here?'

Luckily, one man alone stepped forward. Actually I just sat where I was and shouted, and saved the day. John was very impressed, but manfully, he said only two words. The first one was Thank. I didn't quite catch the second, but knew he was proud of my heroics. I know I was!

John; My web page had told me that the next bus to Portpatrick was at 11.40am, and although this gave us less time than we wanted in Portpatrick, we felt it was still enough time to do it justice.

With 30 minutes to spare, we found our next bus stop and wandered into a hotel bar called '*The Craignelder*'. It was a nice wee bar but we were the only people in it and it is hard to get any atmosphere at the back of eleven on a rainy day, especially in Stranraer. The barmaid was very friendly and made us feel welcome and we enjoyed our first pint of the day.

We left the pub to wander out to our stop in plenty time for our next bus which never turned up. We felt the day was starting to fall apart.

After looking at timetables and talking to a wee old woman, we realized that if there were any buses that day to Portpatrick, we sure as hell had no idea where they left from. Craig was giving me some abuse already, as if it was my fault.

As Portpatrick fell off the radar, we wandered up the main street to check out the pubs. We had been in Stranraer before and didn't like it, but we were wrong. The place is not too bad at all and after checking out the pubs, picked one called the *'Golden Cross'*.

Craig; *There didn't seem to be much of a chance that we would ever get to Stranraer on time, but our driver gave it a good shot. Almost everyone else on the bus was only going so far as Cairnryan. That's where the Irish Ferries leave from now. So it was quite important that they get there on time. We did actually make it to Cairnryan in plenty of time for the ferry.*

If our driver had just dropped his passengers there and moved on straight away things might have turned out quite differently for us. But he didn't.

We arrived in Stranraer just in time to see our next bus disappear round the corner. At least John claims it was our bus. Plan B clicked in and we headed towards the nearest pub.

'The Craignelder' was ok. I think it is more set up to serve meals rather than as a stand-alone pub. We were the only customers. I normally don't like the first pint out of the tap, but this one was passable.

Barmaid Rating 🍺🍺🍺

John; From the outside the 'Golden Cross' looked like an old slightly run down pub, but when you got inside it was something else, terrific. We always go on about what makes a good pub is the staff and the other people in the bar, and we were proved right on that count.

The barmaid Julie was fantastic, her patter was terrific, there is no way I could write down most of it as it is probably not politically correct, as if anyone gives a shit.

Her customers, two girls Irene and Hazel were as good fun and as crazy as Julie, and I remember there was a great wee guy at the end of the bar, called Tommy Johnstone, I think, who played a few games for Rangers in the 50s. There was an older lady with him. I think she was a regular. Getting out and about, instead of being stuck in the house certainly kept her young and lively.

We had a really great time in the pub and I ended up on a table dancing with the girls. Honestly, you wouldn't believe it unless you saw it, which you probably will as Craig took a photo. Julie and the girls even bought a book each, although I'm not sure if we made a profit on the sale, after a discount and buying the girls a drink. Who cares? We had a great time.

Craig got out his magic web phone to try and work out how to get a bus out of Stranraer to anywhere, although we didn't want to leave at all.

Eventually, we said goodbye to one of the best afternoon sessions we have ever had and have promised to return. We both now like Stranraer. Worth a visit any day.

Strictly duff dancing - Sturdy tables though.

Goin' Roon the Edge

Craig; *We didn't have a lot of time to spare if we were going to catch the next bus to Portpatrick, so it was only a single pint stop. Out at the bus stop we began to wonder if there was going to be a next bus. There wasn't. When the penny eventually dropped we decided to cut our losses and find a decent boozer in Stranraer..*

This took us a bit longer than we expected and John made the best of this. I had told him that there were plenty of good pubs in the town. Through the wonder of the internet I had checked them out the night before. This didn't convince John however, and I can't say that I blame him. Last year I had gone on and on about the great pubs I had found in Galloway on my computer. The problem was, they were all shut. Back then, John had taken it badly and made it very clear what I could do with my computer. Just when I was beginning to give up on finding anywhere to rest our weary bones, never mind gargle down a couple of pints, we spotted 'The Golden Cross'.

We were feart to ask her for the money for it.

43

To be honest, I couldn't have cared less what the pub looked like. Just as long as it was open for business. As it turned out, it was a great wee place. Within a few minutes, John had knocked back half of his first pint and was trying to flog our book to anyone who would listen to his schpeel. I was amazed. The customers seemed to like it.

John; We got a bus, number 360, I think, to take us to Girvan, but as we approached Ballantrae, Craig asked if I fancied getting off, checking out the place and having a couple of pints in *'The King's Arms Hotel'*. I was astonished at Craig's instant change of a planned route. It was a brave decision as if anything went wrong with future buses, I would be slagging him off. So in the spirit of spontaneity I agreed and off we got. Checking out the place was easy, a nice garden centre, some nice houses and not much else. But at least it is on the edge of Scotland, so would fit in with our book title. These spontaneous changes in our destinations are becoming more regular. We're really getting to be a couple of daredevils.

Again, we were the only people in the bar, and after the very nice barmaid Chelsea checked the bus timetable, we found we had almost a couple of hours to kill here. Mind you, there are a lot worse things that can happen in life.

Although no one else arrived we had a nice time and the pints went down well. We even played some oldies on the juke box, although there was no dancing on the tables this time.

Craig; *What I had forgotten was that we had written about Stranraer in our first book, and we weren't too complimentary about it.*

The barmaid got to that section, read out the first couple of lines then called John a name I couldn't commit to print. Our chances of selling a book now looked slim, as did our chances of getting out of this pub without a good slapping about the head. Fortunately they thought it was funny and I returned to a normal breathing rhythm.

Goin' Roon the Edge

I really enjoyed the craic in 'The Golden Cross', particularly when one of the regulars Terry, I think his name was, came up the bar to talk to me. What an interesting old guy!

After selling the two books he had brought with him, John was feeling very chuffed with himself. I felt that I should point out that the girls Hazel and Irene had talked him into knocking about £3 off the price and he had bought them a drink as well. The barmaid Julie demanded similar treatment. The financial genius wasn't put off at all. Even when I pointed out that we would have been cheaper just giving them one free copy between them.

I must have been talking to the nice old guy at the bar when the table dancing started. It's hard to believe that people would be at that stage at about one o'clock on a cloudy Thursday afternoon, harder yet to believe that John would be joining in. A young fellow in the bar filmed it on his phone so somewhere out there on u-tube there is a permanent record of it. Any normal man would be embarrassed by this, but not John; he doesn't know the meaning of the word.

Actually there are quite a few words he doesn't know the meaning of. Words like style, rhythm and timetable. It's really that last one which is the important one. How anyone is supposed to make sense of timetables in this part of the country is beyond me. As we were sitting in this pub, I saw a Portpatrick bus coming along the street. One of the locals told me that it didn't actually stop at the advertised bus stop on Thursdays and Mondays. No wonder we missed it. What a way to run a bus service.

On the plus side we would have missed a great pub if our bus had actually turned up at the correct bus stop. Portpatrick would just have to remain a place of mystery to us. It was time to move on.

Barmaid Rating; █ █ █ █ █

45

Pack it in John, She's heard it all before.

John; As time was marching on, we decided to stay on the next bus right into Ayr, instead of getting off at Girvan. We had been there before, and our visit to Ballantrae would do instead of Girvan, making up the trip on the hoof is getting second nature to us.

 Our bus journey up to Ayr was uneventful, although by the time we arrived, after going through almost every backstreet in Ayr, I was desperate for the toilet. Thankfully, '*McCabes*', a nice looking pub was right across from the station and I bolted for the toilet while Craig got the pints in.

We had a couple of pints in what was a very nice, if very modern pub. Unlike many pubs, this one managed to be modern without ruining the atmosphere. The barman was very good and we enjoyed ourselves while keeping an eye on the time. Our last bus was the X16 which would take us right into East Kilbride.

Goin' Roon the Edge

Craig; *On the bus up to Girvan we talked about how lucky we had been to find such a good pub. I think that was when I got a bit carried away with myself. As we passed through Ballantrae I was suddenly inspired to get off and sample the delights of this little town. I blame John for not being sensible enough to talk me out of it.*

It's not as if 'The King's Arms Hotel' was a bad pub, it was actually quite good. Thing is this village pub was completely empty. That never makes it easy to get the chat going. We were lucky that our barmaid Chelsea felt sorry for us and decided to make up the numbers by chatting away to us for the hour and a half we had to kill before our next bus.

Barmaid Rating; R R R R

By the time we caught that bus we had consumed a fairly large dose of our favourite sleeping potions. The journey flashed past, for us at least. We had decided to head straight for Ayr as time was limited. We wanted to catch the X16 which would take us straight to East Kilbride. The last one leaves Ayr at 18.10, so we didn't have much time to look around the town. In fact all we had time for was a swift pint in 'McCabes'. The pub was conveniently situated about 200 yards from our stance in the bus station. I like it when planners put some effort into things.

'McCabes' had everything the weary traveller needs, a decent bar selling a decent pint in good surroundings.

Barman Ratings; R R R,

John; The bus we got back had some problem with its engine. The whole way back it sounded if the engine was racing and should have been in a higher gear. We were worried that it might break down in the middle of nowhere. Thankfully it made it back to East Kilbride, but even at the last minute, we made a mess of getting off at the right bus stop. Craig was sure we did not have to get off at the Bus Station, but could get off on the Queensway and this would save us about 20 yards on the walk from the Bus Station. He was right and we got off on the Queensway, only to find there was another bus stop after the one we got off at, but before the Bus Station. What a couple of numpties we are. This meant a longer walk in the pouring rain. I blamed Craig. These bus stops are about two minutes from our houses, you'd think we would be able to get off at the right one!

So a bit wetter than we should have been, we wandered into our local, '*The Crooked Lum*' and enjoyed a couple, or three pints before wandering up the hill to our houses. We were in fine fettle as we were off to Tenerife on Saturday. Life doesn't get any better than this, does it?

Kate and Sheila were back from their trip to Aberdeen before me and I think we had something to eat before having an early night.

So ended another trip which was nothing like our planned trip, but does it matter-no.

Portpatrick, Stranraer, Girvan and Ayr turned into Stranraer, Ballantrae and Ayr, but we had a great day.

All the towns we visited were great, even on a day when the rain refused to give us a break, and are worth a visit.

The '*Golden Cross*' in Stranraer was the highlight of the trip and should be visited next time you are in Stranraer.

Craig; Ayr, unlike many a bus station, has a toilet you're not afraid to set foot in, and it's free.

We had been worried that this last bus would be very busy and we might not get a seat. Once again we were wrong. There were only a few other travellers waiting for it.

I had been passing the bus stop in East Kilbride one day when the X16 had stopped to let someone off. At the time I had thought that I could use this information in the future. I had reckoned without John though. He didn't believe me. Despite passing this bus stop almost every day in life, he didn't remember it being there. He insisted we got off a stop early.

We got soaked. It was so bad we had to go for a couple of beers until we dried off.

It really is a worry when you think about it. Here is the man who plans our journeys all over Scotland and he can't even find the bus stop nearest his own house. In light of that I really shouldn't have been surprised he couldn't find that bus stop in Stranraer.

Anyway, we had enjoyed our revised trip and were grateful to have to have found the pubs we did. Maybe someday in the future, make that the distant future, we might find our way to Portpatrick.

John; Days' Spends

Bus fares;	£0.00
Train fares;	£0.00
Food;	£0.00

This is as cheap as a trip can get. Just one wee thing left.

Drink;	£24.00 (think I only had about eight pints, but not sure)

Total;	**£24.00**

Just shows you how little it costs for a lovely trip around Scotland. Just take your own pieces, use the bus, and don't drink.

'It's no a bin yer in'

*(Doon the A83 to visit the Crinan,
Several pints later we were grinnin')*

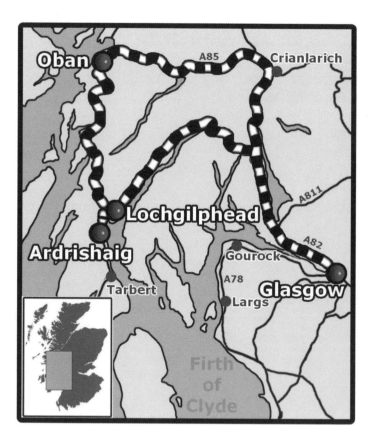

(Glasgow-Oban-Ardrishaig-Lochgilphead)

Goin' Roon the Edge

John; This trip was done on the 4th July, I remember this because we had a book launch for our second book 'Still Goin'' on the 2nd.

It turned out to be a great night with about 70 people there. I had the advantage of having done presentations many times in the past, so I was not too nervous. Craig, and Irene for that matter were terrified. me, being brilliant managed to settle them down and the night went very well. It was Craig who did all the work on the presentation; all I had to do was talk-easy.

Part of the deal with Waterstones was that we would have to deliver the books to some of their stores. One of them was in Oban, which is on the edge of Scotland, so it was an easy decision to do one of our trips and deliver the books at the same time, saving on the postage-magic.

We knew that this part of the edge of Scotland was really beautiful so we were really looking forward to it. We would also see the start, or is it the finish, of the Crinan Canal at Ardrishaig.

There's a great song about the Canal which starts something like this;

Oh the Crinan Canal's for me
I don't like the big rolling sea
The big scary breakers
They gie me the shakers
It's the Crinan Canal for me

It's very likely I made these lines up, but there is a real song, and I'm sure I heard John Grieve sing it many years ago.

I wish I could remember the rest of the song-it was great.

On the day of our trip, the girls (Irene and Kate) were having a day trip to Aberdeen on the Gold Coach to see a friend of Kate's in Aberdeen, so they very kindly offered to drop off the two deliveries of books there.

So back to our trip. We left Craig's and went down the couple of steps and caught the No. 18 to take us right into Buchanan Street Bus Station to catch the ten o'clock bus to Oban.

Craig; I have been in no great hurry to revisit Oban. The last time we were there it was very rainy and misty which is pretty much a permanent condition for the town, if my memory serves me well. That and the fact that the place is always full of tourists make it an unlikely place for me to want to go.

This time, however, it wasn't a matter of choice. We needed to deliver books to the town's Waterstones book store. That's the price of fame I suppose. It's just a pity we were only delivering five books.

The day, as ever, started far too early. John appeared at my front door at about seven o'clock. Since the Queen was visiting Glasgow as part of her diamond jubilee celebrations, we thought it might be an idea to give ourselves plenty of time to catch our bus to Oban.

The number 18 First Bus is not the most comfortable of buses, but we didn't mind because we knew we would soon be getting into the much better upholstered Citylink Coach for our run up to Oban.

As we passed through Bridgeton Cross, I was really impressed to note that the locals had decided to pull out all the stops to celebrate HRH's Jubilee by flying Union Jacks from many of the buildings. I'm not quite sure what the English flag, or for that matter the Ulster one have to do with marking Lizzie's 60 years of reigning over us, but it was all very colourful. She would be touched I'm sure.

John; The trip was livened up by a real character of a woman (Irene won't allow me to say what I really thought of this thing) came onto the bus and started shouting (she thought she was talking) to two other women she didn't know. When she heard they were on their way home to Kilmanock, she asked them if they knew this woman, I forget her name, who she had chibbed and beaten up the last time she was in jail.

Glasgow's great for meeting people like that. We call them real characters. It's politically incorrect to say what you really think about them, and definitely not when they might hear you. This thing was really scary.

When we reached Glasgow Cross, the driver came out of his cab and told us all that George Square was shut as the Queen (God bless her) was visiting Glasgow and there was going to be a concert in the square later that day.

I said to Craig that we should cancel our trip and go and see the Queen instead. He said no (or something like that). I was only kidding but it's great to get a reaction from my left wing pal.

As usual I had arranged the transport and Craig the places we would be visiting during the trip. This means pubs. Craig immediately said that if we missed the bus to Oban it would be my fault. It's like travelling with a five year old!

The bus driver made a call and announced that we were going a wee detour and not to worry, we would all get to the bus station on time. Usually when you are travelling on any form of transport and there is a delay, nobody tells you anything. This bus driver was an excellent advert for the First Bus Company, as if they give a toss.

The scary wee woman got off and we could make eye contact with other passengers without shitting ourselves.

We arrived at Buchanan Street Bus Station on time, and after buying a paper and a drink (soft) we meandered over to the bus stop and waited with a few other travellers for our bus, which was going to Uig. As I am writing this riveting piece of literature, I have just looked up the map of Scotland and discovered that Uig is a wee town on the North of Skye. This is amazing. We are definitely going to go to places like that in the future. I had no idea where it was.

Goin' Roon the Edge

Craig; *Apart from the deranged ex-convict who came on to the bus, our trip down to Glasgow was more or less incident free. Our next bus arrived right on time at the bus station. The wee guy in the high viz jacket who was loading the bus called out for passengers with booking forms to go on first. As usual we had failed to book our seats. When I say we I really mean John, as he is the booker.*

Fortunately there was plenty of room on board so John didn't have to suffer the slagging of his life for an indeterminate period of time. I'm all for safety of course,, but designers really need to think things through before they install equipment. The seat belts on this vehicle were almost impossible to fasten for me anyway. I struggled with it for a good five minutes before giving up and getting John to fasten it for me. How humiliating is that?

One old folly and one old fogie.

Goin' Roon the Edge

John; To get to Oban on this bus, which you can't, you change buses at Tyndrum. This started to look very unlikely, as because of major road works at the bottom of Loch Lomond, (someone was cutting the grass verge,) we were running about 20 minutes late. At least this cheered Craig up as he could blame me if we missed the next bus. When we got to Tyndrum, our next bus was waiting for us no problem. Craig pretended he was happy it was there.

The run into Oban was very nice and the weather, which had a crap forecast for most of Scotland, was starting to brighten up in the Oban area.

I had my pieces on the bus, corned beef as usual. They were great. The only problem was the quality of the tin foil, which seemed to disintegrate as soon as you touched it. I had to eat all my pieces in one unwrapping, sitting on the bus.

I must try and tactfully tell Kate not to buy the tin foil in the pound shop. Earlier, on our first bus, I had shared a lot of wee extras I had with Craig. These included crisps, strong mints and chocolate raisins. To be fair to Craig, later in the day he gave me a Bounty Bar and half of his Chicken Satay. Irene gives Craig some magic wee treats.

Oban is a place that neither Craig nor I like very much, but I think it is because any time we have been there in the past it has been raining or blowing a gale. Today was different. After a few spots of rain when we got off the bus, the sun came out and we discovered that we did like Oban and the beautiful setting it is in. I don't think we could see it on previous visits.

After checking all the stops at the bus station without finding any mention of our next bus, we were enjoying the sun so much we forgot all about it and set off to find the Waterstones store and deliver our books. This done we wandered along the scenic front and found what looked from the outside like a nice place called *The Harbour Inn*. Inside it was not at all to our taste and the barmaid was just so so.

It was while we were enjoying our pint that Craig reminded me that when he went into the web to check my bus times, he got different times from me, so he whipped out his magic web phone and found out that there was no 2.45pm bus as I had found, but that we had just missed the bus at 1.45pm and the next bus was not until 3.45pm. I told him he was talking nonsense or something like that, so he went into the West Coach timetable on his phone and claimed to get the same result. I was sure that I was right, but Craig was not to be put off and a constant stream of abuse at my ability to organize bus times commenced.

Chic French bistro, I think not!

Craig; It was only after we had been delayed on the trip up past Loch Lomond, caused by road works and a driver who didn't seem to know how to work the ticket machine, that John informed me of a little problem. It seemed we had to change buses at Tyndrum. We had lost about 15 minutes and of course I became convinced that we were never going to make it. This wasn't the last timetable problem I had on this trip. It wasn't even the most annoying one.

Anyway the Tyndrum bus waited for us, once again denying me the chance to make John's life miserable. The second bus took us through some of the best scenery in Scotland. This whole journey, delays and bus changes included, is worth taking just for the scenery of the last few miles. The bus station in Oban has a very odd layout. In fact it's not really a bus station at all. It's really just five bus shelters at the side of the road. We spent a pleasant 10 minutes searching the timetables at the 'station' before deciding that we were in the wrong place. The only answer we could come up with was to visit the Tourist Information Office, easier said than done however. It's been moved. That's the kind of information us tourists would really appreciate.

Giving up on finding it we decided to deliver the books. The young chap in Waterstones was very pleasant and helpful. We would both recommend a visit there, especially if you fancy buying a copy of a very interesting book on cheap travel opportunities in Scotland.

John; We left the pub in sunshine and decided to go into the West Coach offices which we just happened to be passing. They were shut for lunch. This is to be expected in the middle of summer in one of Scotland's main tourist resorts and 'The Gateway to the Isles'.

To put in the time till the 2.45pm bus was supposed to leave, we went into a non tourist type pub called *The Clarendon Hotel* and enjoyed another pint in the type of pub we prefer. An old fashioned place with good atmosphere and locals instead of tourists inhabiting the place talking about football and the problems Rangers have. Riveting!

The day was starting to get better. We wandered out and round to the bus stop and there was our bus, the number 423 sitting waiting to take us to Ardrishaig at 2.45pm, as I had planned.

Craig still kept going on about him being right and is planning to write to the bus company about their timetables. I was enjoying myself, but in a non-slagging way.

The journey to Ardrishaig is one of the nicest and most scenic in Scotland, and the sun shining made it even better. Craig was even enjoying himself despite his rage with the bus companies.

I think at some stage in the journey I must have drifted off to sleep, because suddenly I was nearly on the floor of the passageway of the bus. Craig was killing himself laughing. Some people are easily pleased.

Craig; We now needed a bit of refreshment, so we strolled along to a pub called 'The Harbour Bar'. It looked very traditional and welcoming. It wasn't. Actually it wasn't too bad, just not what we were looking for. While sitting at the bar, we got into an animated discussion about timetables. John had planned this journey with great care, allegedly. But according to my super phone, the bus he planned for us did not exist. The actual bus was an hour later than he had thought. I was very understanding, as you can imagine. Since we had a bit more time on our hands to savour the delights of Oban, I suggested a pub across the road.

Barman Rating; 🍺🍺

I had been in there years ago and it had been quite good. The 'For Sale' sign on the wall suggested that I had perhaps left it a little too long between visits. We instead made our way back along past the 'bus station' to 'The Clarendon Hotel'. It's an old building which has been painted in some very vibrant colours. In fact it is quite possible that the colour scheme was chosen by a seriously colour blind designer. It's a crime against art to put these colours together in one place. The funny thing is 'The Clarendon' is a great wee bar. A bit rough round the edges it has to be said, but great just the same. It's the kind of place we both like. The customers, all locals we think, were really enjoying the patter. I re-checked the timetable for our next bus. It still said there was no 14.35pm bus to Ardrishaig.

Barman Rating; RRRR

Just to humour him I suggested to John that we look outside for his phantom bus. I was more than a little surprised to see it just sitting there. John was insufferable on the journey south. He only let up when he fell asleep. I have since found out that the timetable changes when the schools are on holiday. Someone might like to inform Traveline Scotland of this crucial piece of information. Getting this right would help avoid arguments, slagging matches and of course the occasional death threat between travelling companions.

Locked up in Ardrishaig

John; We arrived at Ardrishaig and walked along to the start of the Crinan Canal to have a look at it and the locks. It's a man thing. It was lovely and just as we were about to leave a yacht sailed round the Harbour wall and into the lock. So we spent half an hour or so watching the Lock Keeper do his thing and get the yacht safely through the lock into the canal itself. It was very enjoyable. I still don't fully understand how locks work, but I don't care, it's great to watch, especially with the sun shining.

Ardrishaig itself is a lovely place, possibly some of the buildings are a wee bit run down looking, but that's normal nowadays with the recession and everything, but the location of the place makes up for that.

After all this excitement, we needed a refreshment to calm our nerves, so we wandered back along the front, enjoying the scenic grandeur.

Craig had, as usual been on Google street view and confidently said there was a nice looking pub called *The Slainte Bar* at the end of the row of shops. We had a quick look at it and I decided it was shut, and anyway, I thought it looked like a dump, but just because Craig had picked it.

By a strange coincidence, Kate and I spent our 40th anniversary weekend a couple of weeks later in this area, and were walking from Lochgilphead to Ardrishaig along the Crinan Canal. The walk ended behind this pub, which was open and looked great.

Inside we went and what a great wee pub it was. The owners, Tommy and Allison are great company and I would advise anyone in the area to pop in. You'll have a great time. Not going to tell Craig yet cause he'll just slag me for not checking it out the first time.

Anyway, back to the trip. The next pub we came to was *The Lorne.* As quite often happens at that time of day, we were the only people in, but it was a very nice wee bar and the barmaid, Sarah, made us very welcome and we had a great time and a couple of pints. I was still unsure about the workings of Locks and asked Sarah if she had any idea. She hadn't.

An interesting thing we discovered (but only for me) is that Sarah is leaving Ardrishaig and moving to Glasgow. She is looking at a flat in Holmlea Road where my Aunt May lived for many years. As I said, only interesting to me.

As we had to catch the 4.30pm number 421 West Coach Bus to Lochgilphead, we said a fond farewell to Sarah. Craig had taken her picture and promised her it would be in the book. Craig would promise a good looking girl anything.

Sarah serving up the beers in Ardrishaig.

Craig; The trip down to Ardrishaig was really great as the scenery is fantastic. I was so impressed with it that I described it to John when he eventually woke up. The route the bus takes is a wee bit complicated as it retraces its steps when it goes to small rural communities. However, this just makes things better. All this however is a bit dependent on it being a nice sunny day; then again everywhere looks much better when the sun shines on it. We both wanted to see the beginning of the Crinan Canal. I had driven through this area many years ago and had managed to miss seeing it. How I could do that I have no idea since you actually drive over the canal to get down to Campbeltown. Anyway, we spent quite a bit of time taking photos down at the canal's sea lock. I really think this qualifies as a major piece of sightseeing. It exhausted us so much that we needed a quick couple of refreshments. Luckily 'The Lorne' was open nearby.

The bar was typical of a small Scottish seaside town, that is to say, a bit down at the heel. There's nothing wrong with that of course, so long as the place is kept clean and tidy, and that was the case in 'The Lorne'. We had just enough time for a couple of pints before our next bus was due. Considering how out of the way Ardrishaig is, at the top end of a peninsula, the bus timetable is a wee bit generous now and again.

Our bus up to Lochgilphead was due about 3.00pm, but there was another about three minutes later. There must be a reason for this glut of buses but we couldn't make any sense of it. Then again we did check this out on my now discredited super phone, so there's every chance that there is no such bus.

Barmaid Rating; 🍺🍺🍺🍺

John; We got on the bus, and before we could say where we were going, the driver told us he was only going to the Co-op. I thought this was great. Luckily, we knew where the Co-op was in Lochgilphead and told the driver this would be fine. Wonder what happens if a tourist gets on the bus? Probably never happens.

Lochgilphead is, as the name suggests, at the head of the loch, and the look of the place changes with the tide. If the tide is out, as it was, the place does not look as nice as the tide goes out for miles and the bottom it uncovers is not very nice looking. The town itself is, like most small out of the way places, a bit in need of a lick of paint, but apart from that, Lochgilphead is fine and the people are great.

We visited two pubs in the town, the first was called *The Victoria*. It was a bit run down looking but had a great atmosphere. The barmaid was friendly and dancing around to country and western music. It was great. Because of the time restraints in trying to visit as many places as possible, we could only have one pint before wandering around to have a look at the town and pop into our second pub, *The Comm*. When we went in I had planned to ask the barman what the name meant, but I forgot all about it. *The Comm* is a great pub with a great atmosphere and friendly locals and a helpful barman. Like the previous pub and the one in Ardrishaig, they are well worth a visit to enjoy the banter and a cup of tea, coffee, or a pint, if you want.

Unique photo opportunity, Craig outside an open pub!

Craig; In Lochgilphead we made straight for 'The Victoria'.

63

Goin' Roon the Edge

This was another trip down memory lane for me as I'd actually stayed in this hotel while on a short holiday back in 1995. Back then it had looked a bit run down on the outside and that theme had continued on the inside. The intervening 17 years hadn't done much for the look of the place, on the outside at least. Much had changed inside however, depending on your view point, not necessarily for the better.

John wasn't impressed with the bar, but then, he hadn't seen what it used to look like. It was busy and bright so there were at least two obvious changes from '95. I liked the place, it had good beer and a good juke box, so it was worth the visit. One pint was enough however and then we moved on. On my last trip I had visited a pub which was straight out of the 60's. It looked like the testing ground for Formica! I got fair nostalgic. This time round it was nowhere to be seen. Either it had shut down, or possibly turned into a private house or maybe it had been turned into a museum.

Barmaid Rating;

John; All too soon we had to leave to catch our next bus, the Citylink 926 bus from Campbeltown to Glasgow. This was the last bus out of Lochgilphead that night so we couldn't chance missing it. There was a big group of mainly young people with camping gear waiting to get on. I think many of them were on their way to T in the Park, or something like that. We got on no problem and settled down near the back where, thankfully, there was a toilet.

The driver, Jim, was a great character. As we were nearly at Inveraray, he came on the tannoy and told us, in a very broad Glasgow accent, that this was a new £300,000 bus, not a bin, and we had to take our rubbish with us and not leave it on the bus. He also told us we were stopping at Inveraray for 10 minutes and not to miss the bus or get on the wrong one as we would be stuck there all night. The way he put it across was magic. I wish all people dealing with the public in Scotland were as helpful as him. We got off, and as the public toilet was looking very busy, we dived into a hotel, and as the toilet was only for customers, we had to have a quick one before we left. This was not a problem, and a vodka and coke each later, we were safely back on the bus, with a toilet handy.

It is another great trip from Inveraray to Glasgow. You go round the top of Loch Fyne, over the Rest and Be Thankful, round the top of Loch Long, cut through to Loch Lomond and down the length of the loch. It was a lovely evening and a great end to the main part of the journey.

Craig; We made do with a visit to 'The Comm' on the front street. It had great views of the loch for the sightseers among us and a great wee friendly bar for the drinkers among us. It's a fairly old fashioned bar, wood panelled and with window seats, and my own personal favourite, plenty of bar stools. To be honest it's worth a visit to the toilet just to check it out. It's what we like to call unbelievable. Whoever built it either had a great sense of humour or a complete lack of talent in the design department.

Barman Rating; 🍺🍺🍺

John; Jim, the driver, got us into Glasgow on time at about 9.15pm and we wandered down West Nile Street and cut through to our usual haunt, '*The Horseshoe Bar*'.

As always, we enjoyed our two pints there and then wandered over to the Blue Lagoon for a couple of bags of chips. The chips were the usual quality, very hot, white and soft. This may not sound very appetizing to someone who has never tasted their delights after a few pints, but I can assure you they are great. Craig did have a complaint, which I agreed with. He reckons that the vinegar is watered down. Next time we are in we will bring it up with the owner, Mr. Lagoon.

We got the 10.18pm train to East Kilbride and Craig's Irene came to the station to pick us up and take us home. I've said it before, but I'm sure she does this to make sure Craig comes home and doesn't dive into the Monty for another pint.

Kate was still up when I got home and told me all about her trip to Aberdeen and her delivery of the load (5 copies) of '*Still Goin'*.

On Friday Craig and I are on an epic bus trip to Dundee, Stirling, Falkirk and Livingstone to deliver more copies of '*Still Goin'* to Waterstones outposts in Scotland.

So ended another great trip in some of Scotland's most beautiful scenery. Visiting a famous landmark in The Crinan Canal, as well as some very nice pubs. Arrived home fairly sober as well, must be something wrong.

Craig; *Our bus turned up right on time and thankfully wasn't too busy. As usual, John had insisted on sitting as close to the toilet as possible. It makes him feel more secure. Even so, he was almost first off the bus when it stopped 30 minutes later in Inverary. He's obviously obsessed with toilets. 'The Inverary Hotel' bar is a place we have visited before and this helped us both. With a knowledge of the layout of the place John lost no time finding the toilets. This left us with a good eight minutes to spend luxuriating in the bar. A very quick vodka apiece and it was back to the bus. The rest of the trip was pretty uneventful, apart from the constant door banging of people using the toilet next to us. There was also a small delay due to flooding.*

Back in Glasgow we paid our now traditional visit to 'The Horse Shoe'. Our latest trip had two main purposes; one had been to see, at long last, the eastern end of the Crinan Canal. The other was to deliver our first batch of books to the book shop in Oban.

We had managed both and had a good laugh into the barain. The only problem I can see for the future is whether we can ever really trust a bus timetable again or that useless bloody phone of mine.

Goin' Roon the Edge

I have a bit of an embarrassing admission to make about one incident which happened early on in this trip. When we were wandering around Oban trying to decide where to spend the first few pounds of our kitty money I made a bit of a goof.

I spied what I thought was an up market drinking establishment called The Arbour Inn. To be honest I couldn't actually see what the pub had to do with tree branches but there was always the chance that all would be explained inside. It wasn't.

In fact it was only when I saw John's photograph of the pub, a few days later, that I realized that it wasn't called 'the Arbour' at all. The H had just fallen off the sign.

The thing is John had listened me, or so I thought, when I was going on and on about how disappointed I was with the effort they had put into the fancy décor of the place.

Then again I don't suppose he was listening to me when I tried to explain the simple workings of canal locks; what's the mystery?

John; Days Spends;

Bus Fares;	£0.00
Food:	£2.00 (chips at Blue lagoon)
	Food in the loosest term
	To be eaten only when bevyed
Drink;	£28 (included essential £3.00 for vodka and coke at Inverary so we could use lavy)

Total;　　　　　　　　　**£30.00** (not too bad really)

Note; Buying a drink when you have to use the toilet in a bar or hotel is a Scottish tradition. People in other countries, like England, don't do this. It may be that we enjoy a bevy, I'm not sure.

Big journey to 'Wee Toon'

(Six hours it took us tae get roon tae the Mull,
Dae ye think we'll go back there? We never wull)

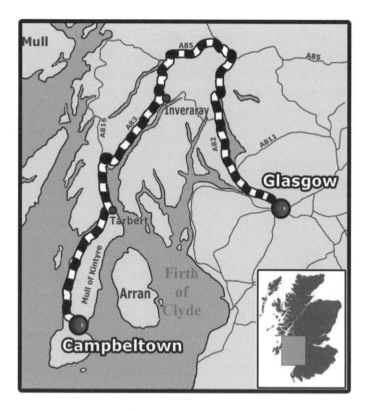

Just Campbeltown-and that's enough

Goin' Roon the Edge

John; This trip was to only one town, Campbeltown. Since we started writing down our rants on paper, Craig has wanted, and tried several times to go there, with no luck.

The last time was on the Waverley, but if you have read our last book (£7.99 from all good Waterstones stores), the Captain cancelled the attempt because of light wind in the Campbeltown area. That's the way Craig remembers it anyway. On that attempt we ended up sailing up Loch Fyne to Tarbert with Craig's pal Tam. Tam and I had a great time, Craig was mad.

For this book, I tried to convince him that Campbeltown is not on the edge, with no success, as it is on the edge. So we had to go, against my better judgment.

The journey itself to Campbeltown will take up more of my story than the time we spent there. There is no doubt in my mind the Gods do not want Craig to get to Campbeltown, well not for very long anyway. I loved the journey today. Craig's version is another story altogether.

So with very little confidence that we might actually get there, I picked Craig up at about 7.30am (that's early in the morning) and we got our usual Number 18 bus. But it was not our usual number 18 bus, which is always a double decker. A single decker came round the bend and we ignored it as all single deckers are number 201s. We didn't bother putting our hands out, but luckily the bus was stopping anyway, and at the last minute we saw it was an 18 and scrambled on.

The driver was a young woman, which some people, but not me, think is a worry. I wanted to ask her why it was a single decker, but I didn't want to embarrass her into admitting it was the only bus in the garage that didn't need reversing out. Craig reckons that comment was sexist, but we need sex in this book to keep up with 50 Shades of Grey and other popular porn.

To be fair, the women driver did a magnificent job of getting us to Buchanan Street Bus Station, parking face in, in plenty of time for our Coach to Campbeltown. Didn't have enough time to wait and see her attempt at reversing, only kidding?.

Craig; This had been a long time coming. We were at long last heading for Campbeltown. Avid readers will know that we have been trying to get to Campbeltown for years now. I had driven to Campbeltown while I was on a short tour of Scotland about 15 years ago. This was quite fortunate as otherwise I would be inclined to think that it was just a figment of someone's imagination.

Every time we have planned a journey there something has come up to stop us. The fact that it is more than four hours away by bus also meant that we would be limited to just visiting the town without a break in the journey for a wee refreshment. To my mind you would need to have a good reason to want to sit on a bus for over four hours at a time.

Many people take this route on their way to Islay and Jura. The Bowmore Distillery in Islay is quite an attraction. I mention the distillery mainly because of something I heard on the bus, but that can wait till later in this piece.

Before that we should consider a bit of Campbeltown history. The population of Campbeltown is around five and a half thousand, which makes it about the same size as my old home town of Auchinleck. Actually that should really be 'old home village', but that just doesn't sound quite right.

Maybe it's for that reason that Campbeltown is commonly known as 'The Wee Toon'. To look at that 'Wee Toon' now it's hard to imagine that it was once a very prosperous and busy port. In fact it has been claimed that per head of population, Campbeltown was once one of the richest places in Scotland.

At one time there were more than 400 herring boats landing their catch on the town's quaysides. And of course Andy Stewart's cringingly awful song 'Campbeltown Loch' could be seen to have some relevance when you consider that there was no less than 34 whisky distilleries in and around the town.

Goin' Roon the Edge

All of this actually makes Campbeltown sound quite interesting, but only time will tell, as the old saying goes.

John; We had about half an hour to kill, so we wandered out of the station into one of these new small supermarkets that are opening up in big city centres. This one was a Sainsbury's and we reckoned our snashters (Govan slang for sweets for the bus) would be much cheaper here than in the wee shops in the bus station. We don't have a clue if this was the case, but in these recession filled times you have to try.

It was all a waste of time as Craig forgot to buy his Halls Mentho-lyptus, or some strange named sweets which taste like shit, and ended up paying 90p for about eight wee sweets, and that was the best thing that happened to him all day.

Our Coach, the number 926 to Campbeltown was a beauty, brand new with all mod cons. Reclining seats and lavies to the fore. We were hardly out of the station before we were getting dug into the sweets. I think I had a wee touch of the munchies after a good night out the night before. Two sessions in a row is becoming too much for me.

Although this was a four hour trip, Craig was starting to believe he was going to see Campbletown, and it was a gloriously sunny day in the West of Scotland. So you'll all know which day it was-the only ef'n sunny day we had!

Everything was going perfectly, I knew it couldn't last. Then it started. We were on the outskirts of Glasgow and the driver turned on his tannoy-oh shit.

Ladies and Gentlemen, he said, as if he was a pilot on a Jumbo Jet, as you will know, the Rest and Be Thankful road is closed today because of a land slide, so we will be going a different way. This is not a major problem but will add around 50 minutes to the journey. We're sorry for any inconvenience this may cause.

The bus was in an uproar, and that was only Craig. It turned out that about 16 of the passengers were planning to get the

71

lunchtime ferry from West Loch Tarbert to Islay, or some other teuchter island, and this delay meant they would probably miss the boat and have to wait for the next one at six in the evening. Nobody knew about the landslide and the road being shut. Several of the younger boat people rushed up to the front to find out what was going to happen to their connection. Their main gripe was why the driver, and there were two of them, hadn't told them before the bus left Buchanan Street that the road was closed. The driver had to stop the bus for about 15 minutes as he and his co-driver tried to settle the mob.

An older lady who was sitting across from us told me that she was going to Islay, and asked what all the commotion was about. When I told her that a lot of the younger boat people were going off their heads, she said, and I quote, 'all this means is that I have six hours less to live in Islay, so it's no bad thing'. What a magic attitude to life, or death.

The driver promised he would get in touch with headquarters to see if they could get Calmac to hold the ferry for a while till the bus arrived, and order was restored. Unfortunately for the driver, the phone was on speaker mode so he could drive and listen at the same time, and the answer was basically piss off.

This resulted in a second uproar, again mainly by the younger boat people, and added another few minutes to the journey.

I believe young people are so full of the 'you can do anything and be anyone you want shit', that they find it impossible to comprehend the real fact of life-shit happens. Our generation, like the woman across from me, is used to this and takes it in their stride.

Craig; By the time John arrived at my house I was raring to go. The bus down to Glasgow set the tone for the rest of the day as far as I'm concerned. There was not one bit of cushioning on the seats. It was like sitting on a concrete bench, while someone takes a masonry drill to the underside of it.

John the navigator searches for signs.

Given the state of the roads nowadays, I'm surprised either of us could walk by the time we got to Buchanan Street Bus Station. We were a wee bit early so we decided to do a little shopping for extra supplies. I bought a packet of my favourite mints and very nearly hit the roof when I found out the price of them. At 90 pence a packet it worked out at 10p a sweetie. Mentho-lyptus must be on a par with gold at the moment for price per ounce. This is a bit of a pity as I found out a while ago that John can't stand them. This has two benefits for me. Since they are too strong for John, I get to eat them all without the need to share, and then of course I get to call him a wimp several times a day. Now unless I can get them on prescription I'll be doing without my wee sweeties on future bus trips.

My mood wasn't improved much by the queue jumpers at our bus stance. Why do people do this? There was obviously plenty of room on the bus for all the waiting passengers. Unlike our first bus this West Coast Motor coach had at least employed the services of an upholsterer. Just as well really, given how long we would be parking our rear ends on the seats.

John; But back to the trip, even though it's more boring than what was happening around us. Craig had worked out that we were now going to be at least 50 minutes late, plus all the extra time this fannying about with the young boat people had taken. On top of a four hour trip it was a bit worrying, although that's not exactly how Craig put it. He was livid. I tried to point out that the weather was great, we had sweets and were going to be travelling through what is, in my opinion, some of the most beautiful scenery in Scotland. None of this helped and I had to almost physically stop him from getting up and putting one on the driver.

The next problem was that the new route took us up past Tarbet, along the very, very narrow and twisting bit of the road up Loch Lomond to Crianlarich, and as the road up the Rest was closed, all the traffic from Campbeltown and other towns in that area had to go down this bit of road on their way to the Glasgow area. The result was that our bus must have stopped at least a hundred times on this stretch of road to let other big loads creep by. It wasn't just Craig who was getting restless, we reckoned the bus would be about a couple of hours late, if we ever got there. And it got worse.

When we turned off the main road to Oban, the A85, onto the B819, which is a fairly narrow and twisting road to Inveraray, we got stuck behind the biggest load I have ever seen. It was a crane on a lorry. Both were on the back of an even bigger lorry. So for about an hour we never got above 30 miles an hour. There were places where the driver of this monster load could have pulled in to let us, and the hundreds of other cars past, but he just drove on regardless. What an ignorant bastard.

Goin' Roon the Edge

The ferry passengers, and Craig, had given up by now and the bus was silent. What was worrying the ferry people was not that they were going to miss their ferry, which was leaving at about 12 noon, they were starting to think they might miss the next one, and that was at six o'clock in the evening. Remember, we were supposed to be in Campbeltown at about one o'clock.

By this time there actually was steam coming out of Craig's ears. He just can't see the funny side of these things.

Craig; *We settled in for our journey, making sure our bag of goodies was within easy reach. I started my first Suduko of the day and John set about numbing his mind by reading 'The Daily Mail'. It was only when we reached the outskirts of Glasgow that the driver decided to let us in on his little secret. The road ahead was closed and we were going on a mystery tour of the Trossachs. He estimated that we would be about 50 minutes late getting to our destination, and like all estimates, this one was wildly inaccurate.*

It might have been nice if he had let us in on this little bombshell before we had left the stance. The chap sitting behind us was more than a little upset. I heard him telling someone that he had a job interview with the Bowmore Distillery in Islay. Quite a few of the passengers were also booked on the ferry from West Loch Tarbert to Islay and they also didn't seem to appreciate the driver's little surprise.

Things got a bit vocal for a while. I would have to say that the driver didn't come across as the smartest guy I've ever met, or maybe he was a bit hard of hearing. He kept phoning his office but didn't seem to notice that the thing was on speaker. We heard every word, and there weren't very many reassuring ones.

John; When we stopped at Lochgilphead to drop off and pick up passengers, the big load disappeared. I've no idea where it went, but it was gone, but it was too late to cheer Craig up.

Strange wee pub in a strange wee toon?

To be fair, when, a couple of minutes later, we got to Ardrishaig, and we had to stop for 10 minutes as the lock bridge was open to let in a wee boat that was sailing into the Crinan Canal, he gave a slight chuckle, or he might have been choking, I was feart to look.

Eventually, we got to the town of Tarbert (not to be mixed up with Tarbet) at about two o'clock (two hours late).

Even then the driver spent about five minutes trying to explain to the boat people that instead of him dropping them off at the Ferry Terminal, which had no facilities, they should get off in the town of Tarbert, enjoy a few hours there and then get a local bus or taxi to catch the six o'clock ferry.

This would also give the numpties the opportunity to sample the hospitality of the town.

Goin' Roon the Edge

The last part of the journey, down the Mull passed without major incidents and we arrived at Campbeltown, at about three o'clock. We had been on the bus for nearly six hours, we could have flown to Majorca and back in that time.

To cheer Craig up so he would enjoy his two (not four) hours in this town made famous by Paul McCartney, I sang a couple of lines of my version of the famous song!!

Mull of Kintyre, O' steam coming out of Craig's Ears
His desire, was to get there and have a few Beers,
O' Mull of Kintyre

He shut me up before I could go any further;
Craig; *When we got up near the very top of Loch Lomond, the road became very narrow. This meant that we were in for even more delays. Our driver was obviously a wee bit nervous. So was I. Some of the big lorries were only millimeters away from my window.*

The road we were on is officially a B road but that was back when it was quite new and motor vehicles were few and far between. Our bus took up about ¾ of the width of it. If I had been cycling along it I would have stopped and dragged my bike up on to the grass verge the first moment I saw a bus coming along the road.

When we eventually got to Inveraray we were more than an hour behind schedule. Some passengers, the lucky ones, got off in the town. But we moved on straight away. Just in time to catch up with the slow moving wide load which had been holding us back for the last 20 miles. On the bright side, this gave us plenty of time to appreciate the scenery. In fact, if we slowed down any more we could easily have been described as part of the scenery.

At Lochgilphead, the driver of the heavy load lorry obviously had had enough of a laugh with us and turned off towards

Oban. To my knowledge there is only one set of traffic lights between Lochgilphead and Campbeltown and that is at the bridge over the Crinan Canal in Ardrishaig, and of course they were at red when we arrived there. It might be my imagination but I could swear that we arrived at the rush hour on the Crinan. Boats were queuing up to go through the Lock. Even when we got into Campbeltown the bus had to take a small detour as a road had been closed where they were re-tarring the surface. I very much doubt that it was heavy traffic use that wore out the original surface.

John; Anyway, this story is supposed to be about our impressions of one of Scotland's more far flung towns, Campbeltown. We were there, but with only two hours to take in the splendour of this famous place. Amazingly, the driver told us that our five o'clock bus back would leave on time, no idea how that works.

I was disappointed that there was no smell of whisky in the air and no mist rolling in from the sea, but there was steam coming out of Craig's ears.

Not to worry, after spending about 20 minutes walking round the place to get a feel for it, and to get the feeling back into our arses, we found a wee pub called the *Wee Toon*. We were by this time gasping for a pint. Why the dummies in The Scottish Parliament will not let us have a wee refreshment on buses is beyond me. Think I will write to my MSP and suggest a change in the law, or maybe not.

There was nothing wrong with the pub, but it was very quiet and the barmaid spent her time talking to two locals at the other end of the bar. She could probably tell Craig was in a foul mood.

I know there will be people reading this who will say that I am always going on about the fact that pubs can be boring in the morning when they are quiet and that the barman or woman shows no interest in making conversation, but that I give you no ideas of my own how to cheer a place up. Well here are a few things a good friend of mine Robin Patrick used to do when he had bars before he recently went into semi-retirement. Robin and I grew up together in Govan, Robin, like most of my pals, grew up a bit taller than me. Anyway, Robin has owned bars all his working life, mainly in Rothesay, with a break of a few years when he had a bar in Newton Stewart. Robin had three bars in Rothesay that I remember, 'The Crown', which was actually in Port Bannatyne, 'The Rabbie Burns' and then 'The Glue Pot' in Rothesay. Because of him they were all great bars.

Some of the simple thing he would do like having papers, the Racing Post and betting slips on the bar so he could discuss the racing at Redcar, or wherever. Even if you knew nothing about racing, it was good patter. There was always a wee old man, who was always in the bar, who would nick out and put on your bet, for a half pint if your horse won.

Another great laugh was the swearing hour. If I remember right, for the first hour after the bar opened in the morning, you were allowed to swear. Nowadays, people's language has deteriorated and swearing is commonplace, but in days gone by, people did not swear as much, especially if ladies were present. Nowadays women seem to swear as much as men. I think it is very unattractive to hear a woman swear, if that makes sense.

Talking about swearing reminds me of a pal I had when I was young, big Bill McLelland, who was a fantastic swearer. He did it without knowing, and put swear words in the middle of words. He was fanf***** tastic at it. Anyway, back to my story, one day Kate and I were in Rothesay and as was my norm, I was in Robin's one morning while Kate did a bit of shopping. Kate was in her 20s' at the time and never swore, except at me, so in she pops at just before 12 o'clock and because she did not want to spoil the regulars chance for a wee bit of bad language, which they would never do in front of women, asked Robin if the swearing hour was finished, Robin said, 'no, fuck off'. It was magic. Robin was only kidding and bought her a drink. She wiped the smile off his face when she asked for a Brandy and Ginger ale. Great days!

I could go on for pages about the things, like special prices for old people that can be done, at little cost to the publican, which can cheer a place up. And just as importantly to the publican, get people back in every day for a laugh. But I am rabbiting on, so back to today's trip.

Local stops for pint halfway through flittin'

Craig; After a wander round the front for ten minutes or so we decided it was time to get some beer inside us. Our first port of call a wee bar called 'Wee Toon'. It was in a row of three pubs. I've never seen a set up like that before. We didn't go into the other two but I'm fairly sure we chose the wrong one. My first thought was that the pub had been renovated in honour of the Queen's Diamond jubilee. That would be Queen Victoria's. OK maybe it wasn't quite that bad, maybe. The walls were wood panelled and weathered by many decades of dedicated fag smoking.

The bar surface had that great worn look you only get from sliding small change backwards and forwards over it for many years.

Since we had been stuck on that bus for almost six hours I felt the need to visit the gents. That was a bit of an eye opener. Basic seems like a very outlandish description of the facilities on offer in that department. Apparently a simple pee doesn't warrant the use of a hand wash basin. The only sink in the place is to be found in the cubicle. I suppose it gives you something to do while you're in there.

Barman Rating;

John; Leaving the pub behind, the sun was still shining and I took a chance and asked Craig what were his impressions of the place. His remarks were not very favourable, but to be honest, and I mean no disrespect to Campbeltowners, the place is nothing to look at. I'm not saying it's depressing, but there was not even a £1 shop, but we did find two 80p shops.

The next pub we found was one that Craig had seen when doing his Google street view thing. Thank god it was open. It was called *The Fiddler's Inn* and it was a very nice bar with a few regulars to the fore. Like in all the pubs visited, the tellies were showing the Olympics, and everybody was watching.

It's funny, we all start talking about sports we know nothing about. There was some sort of cycling with three in each team and when the British Team came on and won easily I was going on that it was because Chris Hoy was unbeatable. Turned out it was somebody else in the team that won the race. Thank God I'm not easily embarrassed and our pints were just finished so we could leave before I put my foot in anything else. Craig made me promise not to comment on anything else in the next pub we found. I said ok.

Craig; *Our next pub was totally different. For a start it was neat, tidy and very welcoming. I didn't personally check out the facilities but John assured me they were not the least bit frightening. We didn't get to speak to any of the customers in this place, or the last one for that matter. I explained this to John as a Campbeltown kind of thing. Being stuck out on a limb, on the road to absolutely nowhere, the locals don't come into much contact with us 'outlanders'. After all it's a hard place to get to, even without nature conspiring against the would be traveller. We didn't have a lot of time so we limited ourselves to just the one pint before moving on. 'The Fiddler's Inn' was somewhere between our first two choices in levels of décor. That is to say not a tired, worn out bit of a dump and neither was it a well-lit comfortable drinking den. It was quite difficult to get in the door. I thought it was just that the door was stiff, it wasn't. There was what can only be described as an obsessed half-wit playing the bandit behind the door. Rather than move aside to let us, or anyone else inside, he allowed himself to be squashed against his machine. He was still playing it when we left.*

Barman Rating; R R,

John; The next, and last pub we found was called *Kilbrannan Bar*. One good thing about Campbeltown is that there seems to be a lot of pubs and all the ones we visited were great. Not in a way youngsters or couples might like, but great for the likes of us.

The *Kilbrannan Bar* was no exception. Although our time was short in each place we visited because of the bus delay, the pubs and people we met were great.

Considering the time it took us to get there, the time we spent was nothing like enough to get a real opinion of the place, so I suggested to Craig that we came back for another trip. Couldn't print his reply, enough to say we won't be back.

So we headed back to the bus, and the same driver told us that the road up the Rest and Be Thankful was still closed and our estimated time of arrival in Glasgow would be about 10 o'clock. Thankfully the driver never heard Craig's comment about his ability to keep to a schedule, if he had, we would not have gotten back from Campbeltown that night. This was the last bus.

Craig; The last pub we went into was called the 'Kilbrannan Bar'. The actual bar itself was only about 12 feet long, but had a large flat screen telly at either end. This would usually annoy us but the Olympic cycling was on so we watched it very closely. Britain was winning after all. We got talking to one old guy. Actually I managed to steal his bar stool and his newspaper while he was outside having a ciggy. It's always a bit of an ice breaker when you do that kind of thing. Once I had apologized profusely we had a good wee chat. All too soon we had to leave to catch our bus. It was sitting waiting for us.

Barman Rating; 🍺🍺🍺,

John; The journey home was completely uneventful, it was a glorious evening and the memories of the morning's delays were fading from my memory, but it will be a long time before Campbeltown is mentioned in Craig's company.

We had a pint in The Horseshoe in Glasgow before getting the last train home. Irene was waiting for us at East Kilbride station to make sure we got home. So ended a glorious day in the Mull of Kintyre.

To finish off I would say that, even with no delays, it is a hell of a distance to Campbeltown, and although the scenery on the way and around Campbeltown is stunning, the town itself is, like a lot of seaside towns in Scotland, in need of some tender care and attention. That's the nicest way I can put it. As my granny used to say, if you can't say something nice about a place or person, don't say anything.

Craig; *Without a large slow moving truck to hold us back we made good time on our journey back up to Inveraray. We even had time for a convenience stop. We found it very convenient. I had, in order of importance, a half pint of lager, a vodka and soda and a pee. John managed a quick vodka and a wee carry oot consisting of two miniature bottles of wine. I sensed trouble ahead. An hour or so later, we were discussing Britain's chances of gaining more golds at the Olympics when John came out with his take on how things were going. I quote, 'Britain's Bikeling team are great so they are'. I'm no expert, but I think the wine had just kicked in.*

Amazing what a couple of haufs
will do for the weary traveller.

Goin' Roon the Edge

Five hours after we said farewell to Campbeltown, and that's forever as far as I'm concerned, we arrived back in Glasgow. Since we had spent eleven hours altogether on the Campbeltown bus, plus another hour getting to Glasgow on the old number 18, we decided that we deserved a wee beer in 'The Horse Shoe'.

In total we had spent about twelve and a half hours traveling to and from Campbeltown, all of this to spend one hundred and twenty minutes in that town. It had to be done. We needed to get this journey out of the way. The main thing now was that we would never need to go there again. Not even if the loch turns into whisky. It still wouldn't be worth the effort.

John; *Spends for the day;*

Bus fares;	£0.00
Train fares;	£0.80 (Glasgow to EK)
Food;	£3.20 (rubbish for bus)
Drink;	£18.00
Total;	**£22.00**

I think this is the least I have spent on drink, think it's something to do with spending almost the whole day on the bus-never mind, the liver has had a wee sort of rest today. Mind you, my ears are worn out listening to Craig moaning all day. Thank God we got there in the end, even for a couple of hours.

Well away in Galloway

*(The Glenluce Chinese were more than a token
Till the cops found out whit they were smoking)*

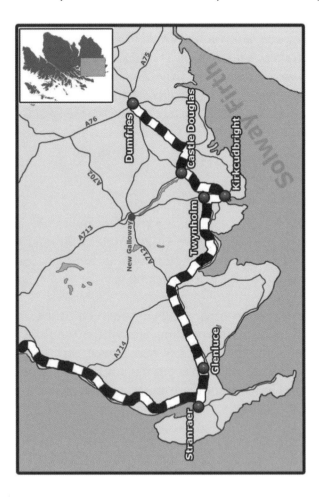

*Stranraer/Glenluce/Twynholm/Kirkcudbright/
Castle Douglas/Dumfries*

Goin' Roon the Edge

John; We had already decided, I think, that the two natural places to start and finish our round the edge of Scotland by bus trip were Berwick-upon-Tweed and Dumfries. As anyone who has read our previous trips will know, nothing goes to plan, but that is part of our plan, or excuse for not being able to read timetables.

I went on the normal Traveline Scotland webpage and worked out that we could not manage Dumfries to Stranraer in one day, that is if we visited the places in between that we wanted to. The places we picked were Dalbeattie, Kirkcudbright and Glenluce. Passing through places is not enough, you have got to get off the bus and visit places of interest (pubs) in these towns, even if it means you might miss the next bus, or get one to the wrong place. Who cares, it's a laugh.

On further checking of the web page, I discovered that if we went in the opposite direction, that is Stranraer to Dumfries, we could just make it. I know that technically this is the wrong way, but it covers the same ground, and more importantly, I don't care.

As usual, the places mentioned above were not where we ended up going, but more of that later.

Craig told me the day before, which was a holiday Monday, that Tuesday was also a holiday. This one was for the Queen's Diamond Jubilee. Holidays are a nightmare for the traveller who relies on timetables. It's hard enough on normal days without throwing a holiday into the mix. So I managed to phone a couple of the bus companies who assured me that it was normal timetables that day. As I usually make an arse of these, this information really made no difference.

We have visited this region of Scotland before, but were not so interested in staying as near the edge as we were on this trip. The places we were going to visit were different from the places on our previous trip. So you can be bored listening to us going on about completely new places.

Goin' Roon the Edge

My wife, the lucky Kate, was away (again) with her sister Sheila (the bevy merchant) and pal Ann on a wee five day holiday to Italy. Ann's daughter is a fashion designer in Italy and they love going to visit. There had been a couple of earthquakes in the days leading up to their trip and about five people had been killed. Didn't stop them though, a holiday is a holiday.

As usual when Kate is away, I have to make my own pieces and try to set the alarm as it was an early start. The good thing about Kate being away is that I can return home without her knowing if I am drunk or not. Who am I kidding, she knows I'll be pissed.

Craig; It began to feel like we were commuting between Glasgow and Stranraer. Down in Glasgow we waited in line to get onto our bus to Stranraer. This time there did seem to be more passengers than usual waiting for the bus. I think there was a large group of Irish people travelling together, possibly some sort of rambling club. The one thing I did notice was that every one of them was holding an A4 sized piece of paper. These pieces of paper looked suspiciously like booking forms to me. Despite all of our meticulous planning, the only thing we didn't bother to do was book our seats. Things started to look a bit bleak when two would be passengers were told to get off the bus as they hadn't booked. There was a lot of gesticulation and raised voices. At one point I thought the driver was going to hook one of them. He certainly looked capable. By the time we got to the front of the queue we were certain our travelling was over for the day. Actually the driver became quite reasonable when he heard our sorry tale. He suggested we go back into the station and book. I thought that this was just a very neat way of getting rid of us. No doubt by the time we got back from the booking desk his bus would be speeding through the outskirts of Glasgow. Not for the first time I was proved wrong.

Goin' Roon the Edge

True, we did have to suffer a scolding from the wee lassie at the desk, who treated us like a pair of geriatric deaf foreigners. She eventually said we couldn't book seats as the bus was full. But when we returned to the stance the bus was still there waiting for us. The driver, our new best friend, told us he would let us on board. We both decided that in future we would always book our seats. Of course that's not likely to happen.

John; Our bus from Glasgow to Stranraer left at 8.30am, so we had to be on the number 18 about 7.15am.

To make sure I didn't sleep in, I set the alarm and also the alarm on my mobile phone for 6.30am. I have never done either of these things myself before so I ended up not sleeping for worrying about them not going off. I have no idea if they ever went off or not because I switched the things off when I got up at about 6.15am.

Kate being away, I forgot to buy the corned beef and had to put up with sandwich spread and cheese. They were really good, so I might try experimenting more in the future.

Anyway, I wandered down to Craig's house and we got the No. 18 at about 7.20am to take us into Glasgow Buchanan Street Bus Station.

As soon as we got to the bus stop, Craig started on about changing the planned route and trying to take in Portpatrick. I think Craig has a fetish about going there as we failed on our last attempt. I agreed he could check the times of buses to Portpatrick when we were settled on the Stranraer bus. Anything to keep him happy!

The roads into Glasgow were deserted as it was a holiday and we made good time into Buchanan Street Bus Station.

There seemed an awful lot of people in the queue for the bus and we were last. The fun and games started when the driver refused to let a couple of big guys in front of us on the bus as they hadn't booked and the bus was full. They started shouting at each other and I thought it was going to come to fisticuffs.

Although they were big guys, the driver was a big tough looking guy and was taking none of their cheek. He ended up telling them to get their cases off the bus and he would let them on if there ended up being spare seats.

We were in a panic as we had not booked and were next in the queue. Funnily enough, when we spoke to him he had checked inside the bus and there were plenty of seats. He was very pleasant and told us it looked like we would get on ok but we would have to go over to the office inside the station and book. This seemed daft to us and it would cost us 50p each but I wasn't going to argue with this huge fierce looking driver so I dashed inside with a pound to the fore only to be told by the girl at the desk that the computer was telling her that the bus was full and it wouldn't give us a ticket. I told her I had never heard of a talking computer, except on Star Trek. She growled at me, no sense of humour at all.

I went back over to the bus and explained this to the driver who ranted and raved about stupid f****n computers. I liked him. He said he would sell us booking tickets for £2.50 each. At this stage we were just delighted to be getting on the bus in one piece so we gave him a fiver, got on the bus and sat on the two front seats reserved for invalids. There were none about so everybody on the bus glared at us but said nothing. By the way, the other two big guys got on as well but didn't get good seats like us. Serves them right for not booking!

I think what is happening here is that a lot of oldies, like myself, are booking lots of journeys they might, or might not go on. If they decide not to go as it is a bad day, or they can't be bothered getting out of their scratcher, they are only losing 50p. I thought over booking only happened with airlines, but there you go.

Craig; I would highly recommend the coastal run down from Ayr to Ballantrae. On a good sunny day there is no better scenery in the world or Ayrshire at least.

Goin' Roon the Edge

We were the only passengers left on the bus after Cairnryan so we got talking to the bus driver. I had thought he was Irish but it turned out that he was a native of Stranraer. He thought our idea of travelling around on the buses, visiting pubs was a great idea, obviously not great enough to warrant buying a book about it though.

The bus to Glenluce was one of those small 20 seater units. It wasn't very comfortable but given the road we had to travel it was probably the best choice.

As soon as we got off the bus I got a very strong notion that things were about to go badly wrong. Glenluce is quite a small place and I was a wee bit concerned that we had once again landed in a pub free zone. I had, as usual, googled the place on my computer, searching for likely looking pubs. Although I had found two of them I wasn't sure they would still be open. The pictures on my computer could be anything up to three years old. A lot can happen in three years.

John; The bus finally got going about 10 minutes late and we had a lovely run down to Stranraer. As we left Ayr Bus Station, the bus went right down the coast instead of going back on to the main road. This is a lovely road and we even went down, or up, the Electric Brae, or Magic Brae, as I call it. This illusion of going up a hill when you are actually going down, and vice versa, is fantastic and well worth a visit. If it was in America, they would build a theme park round it and charge you to get in, but in Ayrshire nobody bothers.

We passed through Maidens and then passed Turnberry Hotel and Golf Courses, which looked great in the sunshine.

After dropping everybody else off at Cairnryan to catch the ferry to Belfast, the driver had a chat to us as we ran down the last couple of miles to Stranraer. I even showed him our first book, but he showed no interest in buying it, although he was quick enough at taking a fiver off us.

We said our goodbyes to him and still had 15 minutes before our next planned bus. When I had phoned Citylink to check the bus times, I asked the girl to confirm what bus stop we would get our next bus at as on our last visit to Stranraer we had missed the bus after a mix up with the stops. She assured me we got on our next bus to Glenluce from the same stop as we got off the first bus. This was different from what I was told on the computer. Needless to say, the stop we needed was up the road on the other side.

On the way down to Stranraer Craig had checked times of buses to Portpatrick and reckoned we could get there and back and still do some of our original planned route, but he was worried something would go wrong and I would slag him so the decision was made to go with plan A.

Craig; *The street was very quiet, but a young chap who had noticed us looking about the place came over to talk to us. We asked him about our chances of finding an open pub in the town. At first he wasn't too sure there was one open at that time, 11.00am. Perhaps it was the note book I was carrying but he suddenly decided to tell me about the Ming Hotel, obviously shut, up the road. He told me it had recently been raided by the police. Apparently three rather enterprising Chinese men had set up a Cannabis factory in it, so much for the inscrutable Chinese. Anyone who has lived in a small Scottish village would have been able to tell them that there is no such thing as a secret in small communities. Through personal experience I could have told them that in a village you scratch your nose in a public place in the morning, by the afternoon the locals will be asking you how your leprosy is doing.*

While we were standing there the proprietor of the 'Kelvin House Hotel' got out of a car and entered the hotel. We took this as a sign and followed her in. The 'Kelvin' is a traditional Scottish hotel, a wee bit old fashioned for some but very nice. The lounge bar was very bright and comfortable, we are so used to meeting owners of Scottish pubs who turn out to be English that we get a bit confused when it turns out they're not. Our landlady here had an accent I couldn't quite place straight away. There was something very familiar about it. Turns out she was actually from East Kilbride.

Like many of the people who meet fellow countrymen when they are abroad on holiday we started reminiscing about the old town. After all I had been away from it for a good four hours. We had a couple of pints before catching our next bus.

Roseann has to listen to John's sales pitch.

John; It is a pleasant run to Glenluce and our only worry was that the pubs, or in this case, hotel bars would not be open in the afternoon. We arrived in lovely sunshine and had a wander along the main street, casually checking out the hotels as well as the scenic grandeur. Glenluce is a nice wee place and we met up with a local called Stuart who was very nice and he gave us the lowdown on all the hotels and their opening times. This was not too demanding as there were only two, and only one opened at 11 o'clock, the other opened at 12 o'clock.

He told Craig a story about Chinese people and drugs in the town, I'm sure Craig will tell you the full story.

So it was into the *'Kelvin House Hotel'*, which is a lovely place with a great bar, and is well worth a visit. It is owned by an East Kilbride couple. Roseann is the lady's name and she is a really nice person and great barwoman. She told us that now her kids are up and away, she and her husband are going to save up and buy a camper van to tour round Europe. Sounds great. The people who run these wee hotels in small towns put in some amount of work to have any success and deserve to do better, in my opinion. Another great thing about the Hotel is that it has a 24 hour licence and the bar can open at 9.00am if you want-magic.

The other hotel across the road is called *'The Crown'*, it looked nice but we didn't have time to pay it a visit.

We said our goodbyes and wandered down to the bus stop and our next bus. A Stagecoach number 500 turned up on time and took us to Twynholm, where we had about 20 minutes to wait for our next bus to Kirkcudbright.

Barmaid Rating; 🍺🍺🍺🍺

For once we paid a lot of attention to the scenery we were passing through, not because we had taken a sudden interest in landscape evaluation, but because neither of us had ever been to Twynholm. We had no idea where it was or even what size of a place it was. I had assumed that it was nothing more than a couple of houses and a bus stop. It was much bigger and better than that. If you were looking for somewhere to enjoy a quiet holiday in beautiful countryside, Twynholm is the place for you. It's also not that bad if you've only got 10 minutes between buses. Once again John needed the toilet so we headed into 'The Star'. It is a nice wee country hotel and we

felt obliged to spend some money in it. There was just time for a swift vodka. We caught our next bus with plenty of time to spare. I had checked out the locations of all the pubs in Kirkcudbright so I was very confident we would enjoy our stay. Then again you can't plan everything, can you?
Barmaid Rating; ,

If you think it's bleak looking from the outside you should have a look inside.

John; Twynholm is a very pretty village and has a nice wee hotel called '*The Star*', and as I was desperate for the toilet and we had 20 minutes after all, it was into the hotel. We had a quick one in the company of the Hotel owner, Mary, another very nice person. This area seems to have nice people running bars, so far anyway. The village also has a diner called '*The Pit Stop*', owned by David Coultard the ex-racing driver. It was shut, but it opens sometimes. This is a bit like the local post office, which Mary told us was the village shop and became a post office on Tuesday and Thursday afternoons I think she said. This is a great idea and should be copied in other villages. The rain was starting to come down heavily as we waited for our next bus, the King of Kirkcowan number 431. Great name for a bus eh!

It was only a 10 minute run to Kirkcudbright and we got off in the harbour square in pouring rain. Thank god pubs have roofs. We dived into the first pub we saw, 'The Steam Packet'. Craig had seen this on his Google Earth Street View. If Google Earth were allowed to take photographs inside pubs, we probably wouldn't have bothered. It was a very drab looking place and hadn't seen a paint brush for about 20 years.

However, as we keep saying, a pub is about the bar staff, the beer and the banter, and all were very good. The barmaid was very helpful and helped Craig with details of our next bus. Craig had by now talked me into going to Castle Douglas next instead of Dalbeattie, as planned.

Craig; The Steam Packet' looked like a good prospect, on my computer at least. As soon as we got through the door we could see that 'The Steam Packet' could do with a good steam cleaning, and that was just the customers. The bar itself reminded me of one of these cabins taxi drivers take their breaks in, I think the word is austere, bleak would be another good one.

Fortunately the barmaid made up for the bar's shortcomings. She helped us find out where and when we should be catching our next bus. Looking back on it, maybe she was just trying to get rid of us a bit quicker. She shouldn't have bothered; we were out of there as quickly as we could choke down the beers. The customers, all four of them, were playing dominoes and getting louder and louder as the time went on. How anyone can get that excited about dominoes I'll never know.

Barmaid Rating; 🍺🍺🍺🍺

John; As we now had over an hour to kill till our next bus, we wandered about the town, which is lovely, even in the rain, and went into *'The Kirkcudbright Bay Hotel'*, and what a good decision it was. It is a lovely wee bar and the barman Neil was brilliant, as were all the other locals, who were as daft as us. The time flew by and the pints went down like water. All to soon it was time to go, but not before Neil and one of the regulars had bought the two books we had with us. Not only are they great guys, but they have great taste in books.

We had told Neil we were now heading for Castle Douglas and he told us his mother-in-law owns *'The Imperial Hotel'* there. This was good information as Craig was sure this would mean a free pint. What a man.

It was with great sorrow we left this great pub and headed back down the main street to get our next bus, the Number 502, I think, to Castle Douglas. It was another nice run through great countryside, although it was coming down in buckets by now.

Craig; We left 'The Steam packet' and strolled round the corner where we found the much more up market 'Kirkcudbright Bay Hotel'. You could tell it was up market as it had carpets and furniture that didn't look as if it had just washed up in the harbour. We really enjoyed this place. The barman Neil was very friendly and chatted away to us for ages. The customers were also great, which was really strange as a couple of them had been the ones we thought we had left behind in the rowdy beer hall that was 'The Steam Packet'. I think we got a bit carried away with things in this bar. Maybe it was the fine company or, more likely, it was the fact that we managed to flog two books to our new friends. Whatever the cause, we ended up squeezing in an extra pint. That kind of thing can lead to complications later on in a day out. That old expression 'what goes in must come out' can get very relevant, especially to John.

Barman Rating; █████,

Imperial Hotel, Castle Douglas. Gary has his lug bent.

John; We got off the bus at the bottom of Castle Douglas main street, which was very nice, and wandered up it in the pouring rain, and into '*The Imperial*'. This was another nice hotel with a good bar with good atmosphere. The barman Gary was really great and although he told us Neil's mother-in-law wasn't in during the daylight hours, she was asleep in her coffin, we had a great couple of pints and a laugh with Gary.

All the bars we have been in today have been great with wonderful staff and owners. This makes a great change from the normal barmen/women who can be sometimes a bit sullen, to put it nicely.

The next bus to Dumfries left from just across the road. It was quite a long journey as the bus turned off the main road and detoured, funnily enough, through Dalbeattie, the place we were originally going to before Craig changed the plans.

This detour took about half an hour and Craig slept through the whole journey, so never saw Dalbeattie, which actually looked like a nice place, with several nice looking bars or hotels.

Craig; Our next destination, Castle Douglas is a bit of a favourite of mine, I have been there many times, passing through, and on several occasions staying overnight. It is a market town and very much a tourist attraction. There are quite a few small art galleries in the town, along with all the usual shops you would expect to find in a fair sized town. Castle Douglas is also known as 'the Food Town', as it has lots of places to eat, from hotels to small cafes. That's the only thing that annoys me about the place. The last time I stayed in the town, food seemed to be at a premium.

I didn't get there till after seven o'clock, but every hotel in the place advertised the fact that they served food all day. Apparently all day means something different in Dumfries and Galloway. Every hotel I went into had just shut its kitchen minutes before I got there. But back to the present, there was a good choice of drinking places to be had but we decided to try 'The Imperial Hotel'. It had been recommended to us after all, and to be honest it was really good. Once again the barman was friendly and some of the customers were up for a laugh.

Barman Rating; ♞♞♞♞

John; Dumfries, like most places, is pretty driech looking in the rain and we had to walk from the bus station up to the train station which is about a 15 minute walk, if you know where you're going. Craig and I have done this walk before, fairly drunk though, so we took a few detours before we got to the station. The main detour was to find a wee 'offy' where we could buy four cans for the train journey home. Craig is too stingy to buy cans in a pub-he's right mind you.

As everybody knows, you are not allowed to have a drink on the train as the Scottish Parliament is worried you might start enjoying yourself. I have a feeling Alex Salmond's a 'Wee

Free'. Nothing wrong with that mind you, and remember, this was not a Sunday.

We got to the station and the ticket office was shut, although there were people in it. For some reason this really annoyed Craig. Some strange things do.

The train was fairly empty so we picked our seats carefully and positioned ourselves so that we would see the conductor coming from any direction and hide our cans. I'm not to sure what the fare was, but I remember thinking it was a bit steep. Don't think we got much of a discount for being old. Our Scottish Government could do worse than giving pensioners free train travel, especially at off-peak times. I think I'll write to my MSP, or better still, I'll sell him a copy of this book.

After about an hour and a half of secret can drinking, we arrived in Glasgow Central, and would you believe it, the East Kilbride train was the one we just got off. What are the chances of that happening, and who cares.

This was about 10.15pm and Craig had arranged for his Irene to pick us up from '*The Monty*', our favourite pub in EK, at ten past eleven. So we had time for a couple of pints to finish off what had been a really great day out-one of our best.

The area we visited was really nice and all the hotels and bars visited were really great. This is an area worth a visit, even if you don't drink as much as us. All the places we visited do nice coffee and tea, I suppose.

Craig; We caught the bus to Dumfries and for once it was me who slept all the way. According to John we passed through Dalbeatie, but I've only got his word for it. There wasn't enough time for a wee drink in Dumfries which is just as well really as we had been well watered all day. That being said John insisted on a wee carry out for the train. I tried to argue against this but he can be very persuasive when he wants to be. Round at the station we tried to buy our tickets from the office, but with no success. The staff were inside but seemed very reluctant to do the job they were being paid handsomely to do. I think they were indulging in that old Scottish sport of clock watching.

After about 10 minutes they crept out of the building and scurried away. This left us nothing to talk about until the train arrived. John is obsessed with the idea that it is somehow illegal to have a drink on trains in Scotland. He insists that we hide our cans in case the ticket inspector sees us. The man would have to be blind, not to mention totally lacking a sense of smell, to miss the fact that we were having a wee refreshment on his train. The law is soon to change making it illegal to consume alcohol on a train after 9.00pm. This would never really affect us as we are always asleep long before then.

The journey home followed the usual routine. We drank our beer and debated whether to go to the 'Horse Shoe' in Glasgow or make our way up to East Kilbride and round the night off with a night cap in 'The Monty'.

The East Kilbride option won the debate and after a couple of pints we declared the day a great success and started planning our next outing.

John; *Days' Spends*

Bus Fares	£0.00
Train;	£7.00 (just a guess-have no idea)
Food;	£3.00 (assorted snacks for bus)
Drink;	£27.00 (pints)
	£3.00 (cans for train home)

Total; **£40.00** this is not as much as it sounds. That's what I told Kate anyway. Her answer, why did you have cans on the train, had you not had enough by then-women-they have no idea.

No smokies ban in Arbroath

*(Up the coast to Stonehaven,
Just to hear a bigot ravin')*

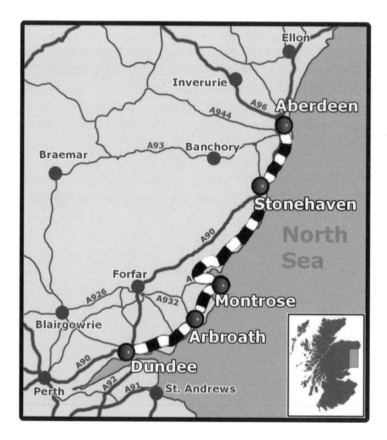

Dundee-Arbroath-Montrose-Stonehaven-Aberdeen

Goin' Roon the Edge

John; This next trip on our round Scotland on the edge, or as close to the edge as our ability to read timetables would allow, would take us up the coast from Dundee to Aberdeen. We planned to stop in between at Montrose and Stonehaven. As usual, that's not how it turned out.

I had as usual, planned the bus journeys from place to place, using our normal Travel Line internet based site. But I am getting clever at this. As I looked at the buses we would get up the coast, they were all the X7, so I decided to have a look at the actual timetable for the day on the web. Lo and behold (or words to that effect) the times on the timetable that appeared were different from the Travel Line programme. I had no idea which was right, so as I couldn't be bothered checking with the bus company, I just hoped for the best and took a mental note to get a timetable for the X7 when we got to Dundee bus station. Like a mental note's going to work!

I had planned to get up at 7.15am to get ready and make up my usual Corned Beef and English Mustard on Plain Bread pieces. By the way, have I ever mentioned that it's got to be Coleman's English Mustard. I'm a creature of habit, most of them involving drink.

Irene, Craig's better half, was away on her summer week or two to Millport, her idea of heaven, so Craig was on his own to make his pieces. Unlike me, who now and again has to make his own pieces, Irene always makes Craig's with wee extras and everything, so I was wondering what his would be like. Would Irene have made everything in advance and put it in the freezer? I don't even know if you can freeze pieces.

As he was on his own, Kate had invited Craig for dinner that night, and as we were having a can afterwards, Craig asked me if I had booked the bus to Dundee and the Gold bus back from Aberdeen. I had forgotten all about it. Imagine that! So we got out Kate's laptop and tried to book the buses, only to discover that the 9.40am bus I had planned to get to Dundee was full.

Goin' Roon the Edge

What a bummer! After a couple of minutes of panic, we found that we could get the nine o'clock bus, which although leaving 40 minutes earlier, arrived 10 minutes later in Dundee. So it was going to be visiting every nook and cranny on the way. Craig was already blaming me.

This meant getting up at 6.30am instead of 7.15am. I told Craig this was not that bad. Thank god I was opening another can of lager for him. This always helps his temper.

After saying goodnight to Craig and reminding him to set his alarm, I made my pieces and got everything ready for the trip so as to have as little as possible to do in the morning.

As usual when you have to be up early you don't sleep well and I didn't need the alarm to get me up. Not needing the alarm was Kate's excuse for not wakening and making my breakfast.

I was ready with my pieces packed and four of *Still Goin'* packed just in case we got a sale in any of the pubs we would be visiting.

Craig was at the door ready and he let me put my stuff in his rucksack so I wouldn't have to carry mine in the poly bag I had. This just means that I carry the rucksack with everything in it. I don't mind as I am as fit as a fiddle, one that's not been tuned for 10 years. Craig's pieces and extras were all packed in plastic containers-what's that all about.

We walked the couple of steps and got a No. 18 right away. The journey into Glasgow passed quickly, we were both reading the free paper you get on the local buses, although there was nothing in it about our new book.

Craig; Today's journey would cover some old ground as well as some new. The cities at either end of the bus journey have been featured before in our writings.

Dundee has proved to be a bit of a favourite of ours over the last year or so, although this time around we didn't visit our 'local' when we are in town, 'The Bush Bar'.

Goin' Roon the Edge

Up in Aberdeen we also broke new ground by finding a new watering hole.

I have discovered to my cost that it is not a clever idea to wire into the drink the night before you are due to set out on an early morning bus adventure.

In my defence I feel I should not have to bear all of the blame for the delicate state of my health that morning. The thing was, Irene was away on holiday and I was left to manage for myself on the home front. Apparently, since I am male and at the far end of middle age, I cannot be fully trusted to take care of even the easiest of tasks. So it fell to Kate to make sure that I didn't starve to death on the three days I would be on my own.

The more cynical among us might suggest that a fortnight on reduced rations, never mind a few days, might do me the world of good.

Anyway, I was invited up to Kate and John's house for dinner the night before our planned trip. And of course one has to be sociable on these sort of occasions. To that end I took a few cans of lager up to the house for a wee sociable drink before dinner. Actually it turned out to be more of a before, during and after social occasion.

Having got a taste for the lager by that time either John or myself, and no one is taking the blame for this, suggested that we adjourn to the Crooked Lum for an informal planning session. It seemed like a good idea at the time.

Early the next morning I could see the flaw in my thinking.

John; The Parks M9 was waiting for us and it was not very busy so we got nice seats and noticed right away that there was a toilet, thus ensuring I would not need to go. It's the umbrella theory.

It was a pleasant enough journey in our comfy coach and as the weather was nice we had good views of Cumbernauld, Stirling, Dunblane, Perth and almost every other town within spitting distance of Dundee.

An interesting thing we noticed in Perth Bus Station was three old men, at least my age, dressed for hiking, and all were carrying huge backpacks. I never realized that guys of my age do this. How they manage to surface after a night in a tent is beyond me. They must breed them hard in Perth.

Craig noticed that one of the guys, a wee bloke, had a walking stick, that although was the normal length looked much too long for him. He then said it would be great for walking down hills. This really annoyed him as that is the sort of shit comment I usually make. It's worrying him that he's turning into me. He'll start talking about bringing back hanging next!

This worried Craig and he said nothing during the final leg of the trip to Dundee. We arrived on time and I amazed myself by remembering to get a timetable for our next bus, and the following one, the X7.

An Irish pub, aye that'll be right.

Goin' Roon the Edge

Dundee is getting quite familiar to us now so we made a point of wandering up a new street to find new scenery and a new pub to visit. This was no problem as Dundee is hoaching with streets and pubs, and very nice they are too, especially when the sun's shining, which it was.

The pub we visited was called *Conroy's,* one of those Irish pubs that's never seen an Irishman, or woman, in the place. Having said that it was very nice and the barmaid was very pleasant and when she found out what we were doing today had a look at our book but never suggested buying one. This hasn't put me off Dundee, with the recession and everything you can't blame people for not throwing their money about. At this stage I got a text from Kate telling me to note that today was a Bank Holiday and to check if this affected the bus timetables. When I asked the locals and barmaid, they all said that it wasn't a Bank Holiday in Dundee.

It was then that my memory kicked in (after a few mouthfuls of Bellhaven Best) and I remembered that today was Glasgow Fair Monday. I felt very nostalgic as when I was young and worked in the centre of Glasgow, York Street, the Fair was a bigger thing than the New Year. Especially on Fair Friday when almost everyone stopped work at lunchtime and spent the rest of the day in the local pub. It was a magic day. Nostalgia is great, but it's not getting us anywhere, which has actually happened in the past.

While I was reminiscing, Craig had checked the timetable and worked out that as it was the same bus going right up to Aberdeen, and there was one every hour, we would have enough time to get off for an hour at Arbroath, as well as Montrose and Stonhaven. So this was the plan.

Craig; John had planned the entire trip, as usual. Ever since I had included a town with no actual open pubs in it on one of our trips John had taken over, with a couple of minor exceptions, the project management of our journey planning.

107

Goin' Roon the Edge

This has worked well, up until now anyway. For reasons I cannot grasp he managed to get us on to a bus which took two hours and thirty five minutes to reach our destination rather than one which completed the journey almost an hour quicker. Maybe he is suffering some sort of timetable dyslexia. That would certainly explain a few of his more dubious decisions recently.

I think we must have passed through every small town and village between Glasgow and Dundee.

Despite still feeling a bit of pressure from the previous night's planning session I made a brave show of it and kept my complaining to an absolute minimum. Even when it became obvious that some evil bugger had left the bus's heater switched to its winter setting I said very little. It was scalding my left leg until I managed to lag it with my jacket. This certainly stopped the smell of burning flesh from making me feel too queasy, but I was then over heating badly and spent much of my time trying to get the overhead air nozzle to work.

In Dundee we decided to find a pub which we hadn't visited before. More by accident than design we stumbled into Conroy's. It looked like a nice place to spend an hour in. As you would expect from its name, Conroy's is an Irish pub. To be more accurate it is an Irish themed pub. It was far too tidy to be a real Irish pub. Everything looked fairly new and just a little bit too well finished.

I remember when a new 'Irish' pub was opening in Shawlands in Glasgow great efforts were made to make it look authentic. Apparently they 'aged' all of the woodwork in the place by hitting it with chains. It was very effective.

I have since found out that only a short time ago Conroy's didn't exist. It was some sort of trendy bar for the late night club going types. Or as we call them, weans.

We didn't get much chance to talk to the barmaid, but we got the impression that she knew her business.

Goin' Roon the Edge

A wee Jakie type of bloke slithered into the bar and started to offer cheap tobacco to the customers. She was on him like a flash, ushering him straight out of the door.

It was just like being back in the Horse Shoe in Glasgow. I've been in pubs in Glasgow when this type of discount salesman has come in with just about anything you could imagine, and some things you probably couldn't, for sale to any one daft enough to part with their cash. Basically anything left unattended or not nailed down could be purchased in select boozers around the city.

It was just after this incident that John decided the time was right to get the books out and try for a sale. Given what had just happened to the wee Jakie with the dodgy tobacco products I thought John was lucky not to find himself nose down on the cobbles outside.

As we were leaving the pub, with our supply of books intact, the barmaid gave us directions on the best and quickest way back to the bus station.

Barmaid Rating; 🍺🍺🍺

Either she was having a laugh at our expense or, and this is the more likely option, we were not listening properly. We got a wee bit lost. John got a bit panicky, but my natural ability to navigate kicked in and we arrived at the bus station in plenty of time for our next bus.

John; When we got to the bus station after our refreshing pints, we were astonished to see the X7 arriving. It was a fantastic looking coach and had advertising all over it letting you know about the leather seats wi-fi and other things. There was no mention of a lavy on the outside of the bus, but it was obvious it would have one as it had everything else, and so it did. The bus even had a name. It was called 'Coastal Rider'. How magic is that? This was way in front of any West of Scotland buses we have ever been on. Craig is threatening to write to someone about the West's lack of classy buses. That's two trips in a row that he's threatened to write complaining about something. On both occasions it was early in the day when he was sober, so he had forgotten all about it at the end of the day, thank god.

A thing Craig said on the trip up to Arbroath that I agreed with was that he reckoned the East Coast drivers were generally friendlier than their brothers in the West. To be honest, this, in some cases, would not be difficult. In the West it's a bonus if they stop. Another thing I find strange is that when you get off the bus almost everybody thanks the driver. Now I do this and I'm all for being polite, but considering how miserable some of them are (I better say a small percentage), I find it all a bit strange.

As we passed Carnoustie I related a story to Craig about a time, when I was a semi hi-flyer, that I attended the final two days of the open golf when it was there. You'll find this hard to believe, but I'm going to tell you anyway how we, and the customers we invited got to the golf course each day.

We all stayed at The Barmoral Hotel in Edinburgh, which is a fancy five star hotel right above Waverley Station, which was running a 15 minute train service to Carnoustie Golf Course. But that's not fancy enough when you've got a few bob.

Here's how it worked;

1; A limo from the Hotel to Edinburgh Airport (half an hour)

2; Wait till the helicopter fafs about and gets ready to take us there (at least half an hour).

3. Fly, terrified, to a landing strip nowhere near the golf course (15 minutes)

4. Get off and wait for the bus to take us to the course (half an hour)

5; Drive to the course and park nowhere as near as the train station (15 minutes)

6; Walk to the course (15 minutes)

7; Straight into the Hospitality Tent

Goin' Roon the Edge

Don't get me wrong, it was a great laugh, and the main thing to remember is that you're not really there to watch the golf, especially when it is raining and blowing a gale, which it was.

I hope you don't all think this story is a waste of time and nothing to do with what the book is all about, but you'd be wrong, reminiscing is great after a couple of pints.

The run up to Arbroath was very nice, the sun was shining and the Coastal Rider was lovely. Although the East of Scotland is lovely, I don't think it's as dramatic a landscape as the West, or maybe it's just what you're used to. It's very nice anyway.

Arbroath looked lovely in the sunshine. We wandered down to the harbour passing a couple of places that did the Smokies. This added to the nice atmosphere of the Harbour area.

Ok John, I think we should leave the smokies behind.

On a topic I normally bring up first, pubs, there were two we passed at the harbour, *The Ship* and *The Harbour Bar,* both were closed. I don't know if they were only closed in the afternoon, which is quite common nowadays, or if they were completely closed. It's a pity, as a wee pub on the harbour front is very nice and atmospheric.

This didn't take away from our enjoyment of our short wander round the harbour, but all too soon we felt we had to try out one of the pubs and soon found ourselves in *The Central*. It was busy, especially for a Monday afternoon, and a cheerful place. Everybody was busy chatting to their pals, so we didn't interact, or talk to any of the regulars. We enjoyed our pints though. The bar itself was not a classic beauty and not one you would pass and say, 'I must try this place', but with only a short time in Arbroath and two closed bars, we couldn't be choosy. Nothing wrong with the bar though.

Before we left the bar, I had the idea of buying Kate a couple of Arbroath Smokies from the smokery (might have just made up that word) round the corner. Kate loves all seafood and I thought that as I was in Arbroath, it would be very nice of me and ensure breakfast in bed for a while longer. I was worried that, as we had another four buses and a train to go on before we got home, the smell might be a problem, but Craig said I was daft and that Smokies are sent all round the world and are wrapped to keep the smell in. I wish I was sometimes.

So I nicked round the corner and the girl assured me that Craig was right, there would be no aroma, and she and Craig were 98% right. There was a wee whiff after a while, but nothing to tempt the seagulls, so it couldn't have been bad.

Before I finish with Arbroath, I must tell you a true story that happened to Kate and I one night at a friend's party in East Kilbride. The party was going great, but at a quiet part of the night when we were all talking, Ian Kennedy, who, with his brother Billy, lived across the road from me when I was young, was telling us all that every year for the last 20 years or so he, his wife and kids had always gone to Arbroath. He made the same sandwiches every year, and they stopped in the same lay bye to eat their sandwiches each year. He was going on a bit more about his love for Arbroath when, just as he was taking a break for breath, his wife, who, like the rest of us, had had a couple of drinks, stated in a loud, but obviously serious voice that she hated Arbroath, always had, and only went because of how much Ian loved it. You could have heard a penny drop in a thick carpet. Everybody tried to change the topic, someone started to sing, but it was no good, the party was ruined.

The next time I saw Ian was when I bumped into him in Buchanan Street where his wife ran a successful business. It was August and Ian was looking very brown. I didn't like to ask him where he got the tan, but it certainly wasn't Arbroath.

Where was I, yes, we packed away the smokies and headed back up to the bus station. It's amazing, for a wee town like Arbroath to have got a huge bus station. No idea why as there's very few buses coming and going, and talking about coming and going, there was no sign of our magic X7 appearing.

Craig; The bus to Arbroath came in more or less on time, and what a bus it was. It was very modern and very comfortable. Although we were never going to spend more than 40 minutes at a time on this bus as we made our way up the East coast John was relieved, if you'll pardon the expression, to find that it had a toilet on board.

Arbroath is a fishing town. If you didn't know that beforehand then you would quickly work it out as soon as you arrived there. There is a definite whiff of fish about the place. I would not recommend an early morning visit there to those of us with more delicate constitutions whether they be suffering from chronic conditions or one which has been alcoholically induced.

We took a wee wander around down by the front but soon realised that there was no beer to be had there. Up the road 'The Central' provided us with what we required; two pints of cold beer.

Barman Rating 🍺🍺

John was going on about how he would have liked to take some 'Smokies' home to Kate. But he was worried that they would stink out the bus. I told him that they were sent by post all over the world nowadays. This seemed to amuse him. I think he imagined that fishmongers in the town simply stuffed smoked fish into a brown envelope and then popped them into the nearest post box.

I thought I had better tell him that they were vacuum packed to avoid them causing chaos in post rooms around the world. The thought of customs and excise sniffer dogs being driven mad by the smell of Smokies in the post had us both laughing, even though we had only had four pints so far that day.

I think any self-respecting drugs lord would have sussed out the Smokies connection long ago. Slipping a couple of examples of Arbroath's finest export into a package along with their contraband, in the knowledge that nobody was going to touch it.

Anyway, John left to buy the offending articles while I finished my pint. When he returned he put the fish packet into my rucksack and we headed out to the bus station once again.

I have to say that just a few hours later I did notice the faint smell of Smokie coming from my bag, so much for vacuum packing.

John; About 15 minutes later the bus showed up. This meant that in our carefully worked our timetable we would only have 45 minutes in our next port of call, Montrose.

This turned out to be a pity as it is a lovely wee town, very like an English Market Town. After a look at the front, which we feel we have to do as the book is *Goin' Roon the Edge*, we walked up the main street and into *The Market Arms*. This is a lovely looking pub inside and out and the barmaid, Isobel, was very friendly and funny. As time was short, we had only enough time for one pint before heading back along the main street to our bus stop. The weather in Scotland for the last few months had been crap, but it's worth mentioning that it was boiling hot in Montrose at that moment in time.

Our next bus, the X7, same as the rest, turned up on time, and we had another lovely run up part of the east coast of Scotland. Stonehaven, our next port of call, was another nice place, not as picturesque possibly as Montrose, but nice all the same. Again we wandered to the edge of the country so we could say we had and then had a look about for the usual type of pub we like, old and tatty looking, and did we not find one.

The Market Bar was old fashioned, but nice, the barmaid Lesley was great, the prices were fine and most of the customers were friendly and a great laugh. The problem was the guy we were standing next to was pretty drunk, I hope, and was the most racist and bigoted person I have ever met, and at my age, and having been to a few Old Firm matches, you know I've met a few. This was just ridiculous and although he thought he was funny, nobody else did, although some of the guys laughed, more to stop him getting any worse than the fact that he was funny. He wasn't.

This was a pity as everything else in the pub was great. As we left all the other people in the bar apologized, without letting him hear them. I couldn't blame them as the only way to shut this guy up was to hook him. I was looking to Craig to do this, I think he has before.

So we went out to the sunshine for a breath of fresh air, to say farewell to Stonehaven, which is a nice place, and catch our bus, the X7 to Aberdeen.

Craig; The great bus service we had enjoyed up to that point let us down when our bus didn't turn up on time. Every minute late meant a minute less to enjoy the sights at our next destination, not to mention the knock-on effect on our refreshment intake.

Montrose is a place I have often heard of but never visited. I have to admit that I was quite surprised to find the town looked every inch like an English market town. It looked very nice, clean and quite prosperous. Of course any town looks better when it's bathed in sunshine, well almost any town. There are a few in deepest Lanarkshire which defy this universal rule.

Once again we decided to take in some of the sights before we continued with the real business of the day. After a good two, possibly three minutes we decided that we'd had enough ozone for one day and headed back up into town to begin our search for a friendly bar.

Things are really hotting up on Montrose High Street.

And that's exactly what we found in 'The Market Arms'. It is a very traditional looking pub with lots of wood panelling and chunky wooden tables and chairs. To be honest I think the place was a little too bright to be realistic. It was no-where near dour enough to qualify as a traditional Scottish pub. Maybe it had recently been refurbished or perhaps its patrons were just very careful drinkers.

116

Goin' Roon the Edge

Isabel, the barmaid, was very nice and friendly. She certainly liked to laugh. Unfortunately she didn't seem to like our books, certainly not enough to buy one.

John had been trying to drum up trade, but there were no takers. Maybe they thought it was some kind of scam as we were obviously from the West coast. There is a theory that east coasters deeply distrust us west coasters.

That idea was shattered when we discovered that our barmaid was originally from Clydebank. Our new theory is that she read what we said about her old home town in our last book and wasn't too pleased with our efforts. It wasn't very complimentary to be honest

Barmaid Rating 🍺🍺🍺🍺

Stonehaven looks like a nice wee place to spend some time, and for the most part it is.

After a quick wander around we chose The Market Bar. As it turned out that was a bit of an error.

To be honest there was nothing wrong with the bar itself. The staff and 90% of its patrons were fine. The one blot, and when I say blot I really mean big mouthed racist arsehole, on the character of an otherwise fine little bar came in the shape of a bloke who thought he was the pub intellectual. He was holding court in the middle of the bar.

This idiot couldn't manage a complete sentence without maligning some group in our society. I think he may also have a hearing problem, or thinks everyone else has, as he apparently felt he had to shout everything at the top of his voice. The man had a solution for every 'problem'. Unfortunately it was the same solution for everything.

I suggested that he was perhaps talking pish, in the friendliest possible way of course.

He didn't take it well, not well at all. It seems that I am part of the problem and would be added to his list of people who needed to be 'taken care of'. I said that doing that was more to my liking than being added to his list of friends, although I did say it in my very quiet voice.

Things got a bit personal when he told me that I needed a haircut. I was outraged as I had just paid seventeen quid for one a couple of days before hand.

After a while he ran out of subject material to rant about and calmed down a bit.

John was upset to find it wasn't free at all.

Much to our annoyance it turns out that this racist moron is a product of dear old Glasgow town. No wonder the east coasters hate us. It seems that he moved up to Stonehaven 20 years ago. He claimed it was to find a job, but we reckoned that he had probably been run out of town.

Usually John tries to flog the books to anyone daft enough to talk to us, but not this time and not to this guy. Besides given his obvious stupidity he would need a friend to read it to him, and that would be a problem. Who would ever own up to being a friend of this idiot?

We actually felt like apologising to the locals for allowing him to escape from Glasgow. At the stop we had to wait a while for our bus but that was preferable to listening to any more drivel being spouted.

Barman Rating R R R,

John; Although the X7 bus is great, the service seems to have its ups and downs. This time the bus was about half an hour late. This meant that we would only have about 40 minutes in Aberdeen. As we have been in Aberdeen before, this was not as major a problem as it would have been if we had not been there before.

We got off the bus in Aberdeen and had just enough time to wander across the road and into *The Criterion Bar*. This was an old fashioned bar and filled our need for a final pint before returning to Glasgow.

As I have mentioned before, the government does not allow us to have a wee swally on the bus and the driver, again a really nice and funny guy, told us that if he couldn't drink, none of us could. There were only about a dozen of us on our Gold Bus service to Glasgow, and we really enjoyed the Coffee, Sandwiches and Tablet you get on board, all free.

It was a lovely run down to Glasgow and we admired a glorious sunset on the way. See what you can do when you're sober.

The Gold Coach dropped us off in Buchanan Street bus station at 9.45pm and we walked down West Nile Street and into our favourite Glasgow pub, *The Horshoe*. As always, good beer, good service and reasonable prices. I texted Kate to tell her when we would be home and she said she would pick us up at EK station. As Craig's Irene was away I wondered if Irene had asked Kate to make sure that Craig got home. You know what he's like, but as by this time it was about eleven o'clock, and since all the pubs in EK shut then, this was not the case and my good lady had done it out of the kindness of her heart. I'm glad

I brought her home the Smokies. They're not very romantic, but it's the thought that counts.

So ended another great trip in lovely weather.

Craig; In Aberdeen we had no time to waste so we headed straight across the road from the bus station to the Criterion Bar. It is another traditional Scottish pub.

Actually it looks a lot classier on the outside than it does on the inside, but it's still quite good though. It was pretty busy as you would expect at that time of day and being just across from the bus station.

Usually these kind of places are a bit on the crappy side. They are usually full of men who have just enough time for a quick pint before they catch a bus home, or maybe they are barred from all the decent pubs in town. Whatever the reason for being there they don't tend to attract a local clientele. This would explain the lack of atmosphere in the place.

We enjoyed our beers and took the opportunity to use the pub's facilities. I'm delighted to report that the Criterion's still offer paper towels to its patrons.

Those pathetic hand driers which blow air just above room temperature so weakly that you end up drying your hands on the sleeves of your shirt really annoy me. Give me good old fashioned paper towels any day.

The journey back down on the Gold bus was, as usual, great. I think we only woke up for the tea and sandwiches. After a quick pint in Glasgow we headed back up to East Kilbride.

The only incident of note was that at the very last moment I remembered the Smokies were still in my rucksack. John had forgotten all about them.

Since I'm not known for my neatness and Irene wasn't at home to check up on things, that bag could well have been thrown into the back of my cupboard where it would have stayed for who knows how long. I dread to think what kind of environmental health hazard might have been created.

John; *Days' Spends;*

Bus fares;	£0.00
Food;	£5.00 Smokies for Kate so shouldn't really count)
Snacks;	£3.00 for rubbish to eat on bus)
Drink;	£27.00
Total;	**£35.00**

Sometimes I forget to mention the snacks I buy for bus, but I always do. Only £27 on bevy. Getting quite sensible in my old age.

To the Kingdom we come

(Kirkcaldy, is really a nice wee toon
Pity it's built the wrang way roon)

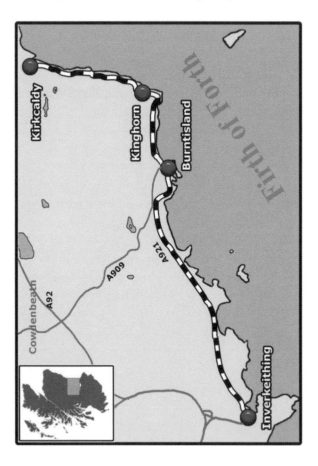

Inverkeithing-Burntisland-Kinghorn-
Kirkcaldy

Goin' Roon the Edge

John; I thought this trip would be a bit boring, as the places we were visiting did not sound very exciting, but you never know. So it was with an open, Craig would say empty mind, that I planned this part of our trip round the edge of Scotland.

I decided to completely change the sort of day it was going to be by having pan bread with sandwich spread instead of my usual corned beef on plain bread. I felt I was getting stale! Some of you may think that sandwich spread is the sort of thing children have on their pieces, and you would be right, but I like it, ok.

With my pieces and some fancies packed, got to try and keep up with the things Irene puts in Craig's bag, I wandered down the hill for Craig at 7.45am in time to catch our usual number 18 to take us into the bus station in Glasgow.

The only thing of note on our usual trip through the east end of Glasgow was Craig's delight at getting two packets of his usual disgusting Mentholyptus (no idea of the spelling, or the real word) for less than he paid for one packet on our last trip. He is easily pleased.

We did not have much time to spare when the bus eventually pulled into Buchanan Street Bus Station, but our bus to Dunfermline, the 9.10am to St. Andrews, was waiting at the next stop to the one the No. 18 arrived at, so no problem. We had time to get a Sun Newspaper to see if we were in it, (it's a long story). But we weren't.

So we settled into our nice coach for our trip to Dunfermline, where we changed buses to the No. 55 to take us to Inverkeithing. Just before our bus was due, another one arrived which was going somewhere else and for some reason Craig thought that as it was almost time for our bus, we should take it. Thank God I overruled him. Our bus arrived on time and dropped us off safely in Inverkeithing. One up to me!

Goin' Roon the Edge

Craig; *On our continuing journey around the edge of Scotland we decided it was time to investigate a much overlooked area on the East coast.*

Once again John was in charge of the planning, and since there wasn't much of that to be done, I had every confidence in his abilities.

He managed to find four towns I had never visited before, so I had no idea what to expect. As it's stuck in the bottom corner of Fife it's an area of Scotland which is very easily bypassed.

I had of course heard of Kirkcaldy before but I didn't imagine that it was much of a tourist hot spot.

Kirkcaldy is most famous for the manufacture of linoleum and while I don't know the exact procedure for making the stuff, I'm fairly certain that it is a messy and very smelly business. Two of the least appealing tourist attractions I can think of.

Inverkeithing doesn't at first sound like much of an exciting destination either. I had of course checked out the place on Google but I think it must have been a very over cast day when the town was photographed, It looked rather dull. There seems to be a fair bit of industry, or at least industrial buildings at the edge of the town which once again tends not to attract the tourist pound.

The other two towns we were going to visit, Burntisland and Kinghorn, were a complete mystery to me.

We made our way down to Glasgow to catch the bus to St. Andrews but our minds were not on the job in hand. A week before this trip we had been on an altogether different type of trip.

The Scottish Sun had heard of our little adventures and one of their feature writers had decided to do a little 'piece' on us. John was thrilled of course, but I was a little more cautious about the whole thing.

They had the idea that we should re-enact the scenes from the television series 'Still Game' where the two main characters visit a distillery.

For some reason many people think we resemble the two main characters in the show. That's annoying, but up until now that is all it was. Now that the 'Sun' was getting involved the potential for embarrassment had increased enormously.

Anyway, we spent the entire day traipsing around a distillery making complete arses of ourselves, followed every minute by a reporter and photographer.

The article, with pictures was due to be published in the middle of the following week. That was what we were thinking about on the trip down to Glasgow.

As it turned out the article didn't appear that day, so all the worrying had been for nothing. We assumed that it would have to be a really slow news day before we got to grace the centre pages of the newspaper.

Michael Joseph John Gallagher,
just one of the bhoys.

Goin' Roon the Edge

John; It was dry but dull, and Inverkeithing looked pretty dreich and depressing. However, seasoned travellers that we are, we were not put off by first impressions and after finding our stop for the next bus, had a wander round the town. Craig had originally wanted to get a wee local bus down to the Forth Bridge to take a photo, thank goodness he didn't. When we eventually saw the bridge, half of it was covered in mist.

In a back street we found our first pub. It was called *Gallaghers.* In we went and what a great pub it was. The barman and the regulars were great company. It was a real Celtic pub, strips and memorabilia everywhere. But the barman, whose name was something like John, Joseph, Paul and some other Pope's name was a great guy and welcomed any football fans in, even the bluenoses.

He told us an interesting fact that before the Gallaghers bought the pub, it was a Masonic place with secret writing above the door. The secret writing is still there but it was very hard to read. I think it said something about the Pope! But I'm not sure I want to know.

We had a couple of pints, a great time and were sorry when we were forced to leave by father time.

We did not have much time left, but we nicked into *The Burgh Arms,* which was the complete opposite type of pub, very quiet, with more like the golfing set spread around the place. It was a nice pub in a more sober way.

Leaving the pub, we walked across the road, almost getting knocked down by a milk lorry, and got our next bus, the 57, which took us on the half hour journey to Burntisland.

Craig; We arrived in Inverkeithing with thirty minutes sightseeing time in hand before we got down to the serious business of the day. That is to say, the pubs weren't open yet so we wandered around a bit.

I wasn't impressed at first. For some reason I thought that Inverkeithing would have a decent view of the sea or a sandy beach perhaps, but there wasn't even a hint of them. During my extensive computer search of the town I somehow forgot to check for these things. Strange that isn't it?

If there was anything worth seeing it was being kept well hidden. On the plus side however, for a small town Inverkeithing has an impressive number of pubs.

While we were strolling around I remembered one I had seen on my computer. It was off the main street, near the top of the town. Gallagher's on Heriot Street was an inspired choice, or it would be if you were a dyed in the wool Celtic supporter.

I doubt there was a square foot of wall space which didn't have a piece of Celtic memorabilia hanging from it.

Almost as soon as we got settled at the bar we got talking to the barman and his customers. Michael Joseph John Gallagher, the barman and owner turned out, not unexpectedly, to be a big Celtic fan, and a very chatty one at that.

Being a mainly Celtic pub it was hardly surprising that most of the jokes being told were aimed at that other large Glasgow team who were experiencing some financial difficulties at the time. But it was all done with good humour.

The banter was really good and more importantly so was the beer. We asked the barman which of the other pubs was the worst one in town as we like a bit of contrast on our days out. That was probably a bad idea. He told us his was the best pub and all the others were the worst. It really was a daft thing to ask and when I think about it I'm fairly sure it was John's idea.

When we said we were going to Burntisland later but didn't know which pubs to visit the young barmaid started phoning her friends who lived there to make sure we wouldn't be trying to visit a pub which had ceased trading. I think she must have read at least one of our books. We were very impressed by her efficiency.

Barman rating ℞℞℞℞℞,

Round on High Street we entered The Burgh Arms. Compared to our first pub this place was very quiet. It was well laid out and comfortable. But we didn't get to talk to either the barman or any of his customers. The pub looked like it catered for an entirely different crowd than Gallagher's, which was as good a reason as any to make this a short visit.

Barman Rating

John promised me a meal and a show, but this was ridiculous.

John; The countryside in this area is nice, but not very dramatic, and this was the same for the rest of our journeys that day. But back to the important part of the trip-the bevy.

Getting off in the centre of the town, Craig was excited when he saw the shows were in town. Being brought up in Auchinleck, he never saw much of the wilder side of life. Fortunately, the place looked very quiet and we decided to wander round the town and down to the front. We were trying to find a pub called *The Smugglers,* which we were told by the guys in *Gallagher's* was the best pub in town. We found it, it was shut. To be honest there is not much else to see in this part of town, and after getting lost and having to go through the train station to get back to the High Street, we found a pub that was open, *'The Silver Tassie'.*

Gillian and Sandy from the Old Port, Burntisland.

This was not much of a bar with no atmosphere and no one to talk to, so we finished our pints and wandered back up the High Street. Craig was sensing the smell of Creich (Auchinleck for Lard), which meant a Chip Shop was near. We found it by smell and went in and got a couple of bags of chips. They were not bags, but trays, and you got a wee fork so your hands didn't get covered in brown sauce. We sat outside the shows and enjoyed our chips while deciding what pub to visit next.

We chose the wrong one. *The Golf Tavern* was a bit of a dump. The barman spent the time we were in playing himself at darts. Hope he lost.

Things then improved dramatically. We wandered up to the cross and into a great pub called *The Old Port.* This is what a pub should be like. The barmaid Gillian and the owner Sandy were great company, as were the regulars. We told them what we were doing and showed them our two books. Sandy bought them both and said he would keep them in the bar for the regulars to read. We had a great time and overran our departure time by quite a lot, I think. We eventually left and got a later bus to our next port of call on the edge, Kinghorn.

Craig; Burntisland was our next stop and it also benefitted from a generous number of drinking establishments. Unfortunately the one which had been recommended to us was no longer one of them. The Smuggler's which Gallagher's barmaid had told us was not to be missed was shut. So much for little miss efficiency.

To make matters worse it had been particularly hard to find as it was hidden down near the front in what turned out to be a very long cul-de-sac.

We found the pub's sign lying face down in the car park. I said to John, "That's not a good sign!" He didn't get it, but then he rarely does.

On the plus side we did get to see a fair bit of the town as we tried to find our way back up to the main street. The minus side was that most of what we saw was an eyesore.

Back on High Street we passed a building which must have looked very imposing once. It looked a bit like a church building and according to the date carved on the wall it was built in 1860. For some reason a thing like a badly planned conservatory has been added on to the front of it. Maybe the planning department was on strike the day the blueprints for this monstrosity landed in the office. It's the only excuse I can think of for doing something like this to a grand old building.

By this time we were desperately thirsty. It was time for a drink. It was possibly desperation that made us choose 'The Silver Tassie' as a place to quench that thirst.

The young girl at the door, smoking like a small chimney, was obviously the barmaid. There was no reason other than employment for a young girl to be hanging about this place.

This really was a bad sign; it's hard to get served when the bartender isn't actually in the building.

Even when she did come back inside she spent a good portion of her time sooking the face off her boyfriend, not a pretty sight. We didn't stay long.

Barmaid Rating 🅡🅡

As we walked along the street we were certain the worst was behind us, big mistake.

The Golf Tavern was our next unfortunate choice; we were definitely on a fully fledged losing streak so far in Burntisland. Perhaps we got there on a bad day.

The only thing the barman said to us in all the time we were in this dump was, and I quote, "Six pounds thirty!"

When I say the entire time we were in there I'm talking about a period of fifteen minutes, and that includes a toilet stop for John.

Barman Rating 🅡

Luckily for us we were only a short distance away from The Old Port. This place was well worth putting up with all the crap that had gone on before.

It was bright and airy and the staff were great. Gillian, the barmaid was very friendly and really nice to talk to. While we were chatting away to her the gaffer Sandy came in and after listening to our well-rehearsed routine about what we were up to, John managed to sell him a couple of books.

A couple of the customers came over to talk to me while John and Sandy were still chatting. I think one was called David Smith. They told me a few interesting facts about the town and its history. Between David and the other chap whose name I didn't catch I learned that Burntisland has a few interesting claims to fame.

The one which stuck in my rapidly deteriorating brain concerned golf. I'd had several pints by this time so cannot entirely guarantee the facts of their stories. It would seem that Burntisland has the eleventh oldest golf course in the world.

You never know when that is likely to pop up in a quiz, but if it does I'll be ready. Of course I don't really know if they were just winding me up or not.

Barman Rating ♖♖♖♖♖,

Willie Cunningham, The Crown, Kinghorn

John; It was only a 10 minute run to Kinghorn, and during that time we tried to re-organise the rest of our timetable for the day. As you can imagine, after a right few pints, or in my case, vodkas and soda, (I had changed because of bladder fears) we were clueless as to what was happening, but we felt we had time in hand so we were not worried. You never are when you've had a few.

We almost missed Kinghorn, but were glad we didn't. After walking back into and through the town, which was not too bad, we found ourselves in *'The Crown'*. This was another great pub and the barman, a great guy called Willie Cunningham was great company, he even bought us a drink even though he knew we were leaving after we finished it. We enjoyed our time and the company was great. This was turning out to be a great day.

Craig; I am certain that I have never heard of the town of Kinghorn, but I'm glad that we stopped there. Not just because of the free drink courtesy of the owner of the Crown Tavern, Willie Cunningham. It just happened to be a great wee bar. We always appreciate a comfortable and clean pub. When the barman and his customers treat strangers so well then that is just a bonus.

Barmaid Rating 🍺🍺🍺🍺🍺,

John; At about five o'clock, I think, but am not sure, our number seven bus picked us up and took us the 15 minute journey to our final port of the day Kirkcaldy

On our way to Kirkcaldy, Craig and I were trying to think of the things, or people, that the town is famous for. The only things that we could think of was Gordon Brown, left wing Labour leader for a few weeks, Jim Baxter, greatest left footer ever to play for Rangers and Linoleum, a famous floor covering. I don't think it's called Linoleum any more, but maybe it is.

Goin' Roon the Edge

Our bus got into Kirkcaldy and passed some really nice areas on the way. The bus station is in the centre of town just behind the main street, called High Street. This part of the town is quite nice. The sun was shining, which helped.

Since we are *Goin' Roon the Edge,* we felt we had to go a walk down to the water to check out the view. This was a mistake. The view looking out is very plain. The only thing of note was a big ugly ship in the distance. Things got worse when we turned round and looked across the main road which splits the town from the beach.

The bit of the town facing the front is pretty dismal. If it is not a building site, it is something else equally depressing.

So we wandered back up to High Street and found an Irish Pub (every town has one). This was called *Betty Nicol's*, a strange name for a pub, but there you go.

It was a nice pub inside, and the barmaid Elaine was great. She gave us a detailed history of the pub from 1741 up till the present day. This might sound boring, but when you're enjoying a pint, even history sounds ok. Schools should try this.

Craig spent about an hour getting a picture of Elaine and the other barmaid Ashley, who were delighted to know that they were going to appear in our next book. It's a dull life in Kirkcaldy.

We asked Elaine if there were any other pubs as good as theirs, as we had to visit more than one to get an overall picture of Kirkcaldy and hope it's better than the overall picture of the promenade.

She told us to head down to the *Harbour Bar*, so we did. This was an old fashioned looking pub from the outside, inside too.

The barman, Nick Broomfield was a nice bloke and filled us in on the history of the bar. He said it was the pub of the year in 2000. I found this a wee bit hard to believe, but if you're reading this Nick, I do believe it. We had a great time in this

134

pub and Nick also told us that he brews his own beer behind the pub. Craig was listening intently to the story of the brewery Don't know why as Craig has never tried anything but lager, and only Tennent's, if he can get it.

I think Craig, and maybe myself as well, but definitely not as much, are trying to get interesting stories to put in our books.

The time for our bus home was fast approaching, and as we have found out to our cost in the past, buses wait for no man, or women. And this bus was no exception.

Ashley and Elaine from Betty Nicol's, Kirkcaldy.

Craig; Kirkcaldy was our last destination of the day and I'm happy to report that there was not a hint of linoleum in the atmosphere.

The town has some very nice areas in it but very few of them are near the sea front.

Goin' Roon the Edge

Down there you get the impression that the town planners never actually visited the place at any time before, during or after they drew up their detailed plans.

Maybe they just posted the plans to the developers who simply misread them. It looks like they built it back to front. Usually people try to make a feature of their seascape, if they are lucky enough to have one. Not in Kirkcaldy they didn't, everything of any interest seems to be facing away from the sea.

I mean, how often have you walked along the promenade at your favourite resort and found that the only thing that was open was a carpet showroom?

The barmaid in Betty Nicol's told me that there had been a lot of flooding on the road at the seafront in the last few years so maybe there is good reason to stay away from it. The sea defences certainly haven't enhanced the look of the place.

Betty Nicol's was first stop in the town and it was a really good one. Elaine, our barmaid, had a very peculiar nickname which after only a few minutes we realised she had definitely earned. Apparently the patrons call her 'Gabby Annie'. I'm not sure about the Annie part of that nickname but I can confirm that as far as Gabby is concerned, and I say this with affection, she is in a class of her own.

She was really nice to talk to and full of helpful facts and advice, in fact she even gave us the name of another pub we might like to visit.

We told her all about the book and she promised to get round to Waterstones and buy a copy of it as soon as possible. I believe her.

One thing we had noticed on our east coast adventures was that most of the people we had talked to in pubs there had been very willing to have their photographs taken. This is not always the case. For some reason many people on the west coast are more reluctant to pose for us.

I put this down to either a lack of confidence or an abiding dislike of answering awkward questions down at their local Department of Work and Pensions. Anyway, Elaine, to give her proper name and her workmate were happy to oblige.

Barmaid Rating ♜♜♜♜♜,

The pub Elaine had recommended, The Harbour Bar, was a fair wee walk from Betty's. In fact we thought we had taken a wrong turning. Just as we were about to give up, something we do quite often, we spotted it.

As a rule any business with the word harbour in its name could be expected to be on or overlooking the sea. It suggests weathered, moss covered old harbour walls. There should be brightly painted fishing boats bobbing on the water while their crews prepare to set off for the fishing grounds. It's sort of implied in the phrase Harbour Bar.

In Kirkcaldy the Harbour Bar overlooks a block of flats. True they are new, well-built flats but, it just doesn't seem right. When we eventually spotted it we were less than impressed, it didn't look up to much really.

Thankfully it was a bit better on the inside. We were the only customers, as usual. When we talked to the owner Nick, things perked up a bit

It turns out that he has a micro-brewery at the back of the pub and he has won prizes for his real ales. I'm sure they were really great but since I never touch the stuff I didn't bother trying for a free sample.

Nick told me that the last new beer he had brewed was a bit special. In fact he had run a wee competition among his regulars to find a name for it. The only rules were that it should commemorate Kirkcaldy's past and be a name everyone would remember. The winning entry managed both these challenges. The beer was duly named Lino Ritchie. I thought it was funny but John didn't get it.

It seems Nick used to rub shoulders with some of Scotland's most famous showmen. Apparently Jimmy Logan was often a guest in his house and Lex MacLean was also a frequent visitor when he was playing the local theatre.

According to Nick, although Lex was a great comedian he had another side to his character when not on stage. It seems oor Lex was a right dour old bugger when not in the spotlight.

I think we could have had a few more beers and found out an awful lot more about the faces behind the names of Scotland's light entertainment heritage. But we needed to catch a bus.

The bus back to Glasgow was, as usual a lot quicker for us than most of the rest of the passengers.

Barmaid Rating ﷽﷽﷽﷽﷽,

Nick Broomfield, The Harbour Bar, Kirkcaldy.
The man owns a bar and a brewery,he's got it made.

John; I have mentioned in a previous trip that the East of Scotland bus drivers seem to be friendlier and more helpful lot than their counterparts in the West. This idea was put on the back burner when our driver reversed out of the bay with two old women banging on the door. Maybe he has just moved to Kirkcaldy from the West. Must give the East the benefit of the doubt.

We had a laugh on the bus when a wee woman took offence, in a big way, to the inspector who was on the bus to check if us oldies had the correct bus passes. She ranted and raved at this wee bloke, who didn't help matters with his arrogant manner which made things worse, as I said. What a laugh.

We settled down for our long journey home, again via Dunfermline.

When we got off the bus in Glasgow, we still had time for a wee refreshment, or two, before getting the train to Hairmyres, from where, for a change, Craig's Irene was waiting to take us home. I had an empty house as Kate was away with her neice Julie at the Tattoo in Edinburgh, so she never got to see how sober I was!

Overall, I would say that the places we visited were all a wee bit run down, but the people and the pubs in general more than made up for any cosmetic failings. The biggest town, Kirkcaldy is a no bad place, if you forget about the seaside bit. The people we met were great, and so were the bars we visited. The bad tempered driver was there just to remind us that we are in Scotland.

John; *Days' Spends;*

Bus fares;	£0.00
Food;	£2.00
Train;	£0.80
Drink;	£36.00 (and we got one for nothing)
Total;	**£38.50** (if I didn't drink I'd be a millionaire

Please remember I sometimes spill some of the drink

No 'lock in' at the 'Lock Inn'

*(Right doon the Great Glen past Loch Ness,
Nae sign o' the Monster, we couldn't care less)*

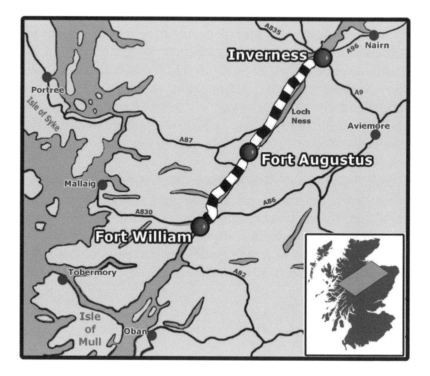

*Inverness-Fort Augustus- Fort William
-Oban*

Goin' Roon the Edge

John; It was while we were having a meeting in the Lum (our local) that we decided to count up the trips we had done and how many more we would have to do to go round the edge of Scotland. This was after a few pints, but even in our favourite mode, we realized that it would take at least 25 trips to accomplish the task we had set ourselves for this book. After much studying of the map of Scotland, especially the teuchter areas north of the Great Glen, or Loch Ness for the non-geographical people reading this, we came to the conclusion that another couple of pints were needed. Once they were settled and Craig had complained about the price, again, we decided that the only answer, if we were to keep the book to a reasonable size, was to go round the edge of Scotland, but miss out the bit north of Loch Ness.

So it was decided by a unanimous decision, after about five pints, to miss out the top bit, but to do a fourth book in our trilogy, and visit the Highlands and Islands by bus, but I imagine a few ferries will be needed because of the 'island' bit of the journey.

So we felt, for no logical reason, that we could still call this masterpiece 'Goin' Roon the Edge', so we have!

Today's trip was a big one, but one that would cover some fantastic scenery and also we might see the Monster. We reckoned that the Bed and Breakfasts in Inverness would be getting quiet by now as it was the end of August, so a sighting would be likely.

We didn't plan to spend too long in Inverness as we had been there before, but it is on the edge, roughly, so I organized at least an hour to check out a new pub or so.

We had thought that when we left Fort William, we might be able to go down the edge to Oban, before getting a late bus home to Glasgow, but this was not possible, at least not in one day. So we decided to get the bus from Fort William straight back to Glasgow. We have been in Oban a couple of times and

141

have done the journey from Ballachulish down the coast to Oban before, so I will now tell you about it, even though it was on a previous journey. This is called journalistic license.

This is a lovely part of our coastline and during the journey you pass very small hamlets. The amazing thing is that they all have many lovely, and substantial churches, but very few people. There must have been some very wealthy and scared Christians in these days who thought they could buy their way through the golden gates by the use of cheap local labour.

There is also a great cycle path beside most of the road and Craig reckoned it looked like one of the best and most scenic paths he had seen. It was also pretty flat, which helps. The journey ends with the crossing of the single track, but very iconic looking Connel Bridge. This part of the edge is extremely scenic and definitely worth a trip.

Craig; We don't often find ourselves admitting defeat when it comes to travel planning. That's usually because we just pretend that whatever happens is what we meant in the first place. It's a flawed system but it's a system that works for us. Or it did up until now.

The whole concept of this book was for us to travel in a continuous line around the coast of Scotland. Each stretch of that journey would be completed in a single day with us returning to the last stopping point a few weeks later to restart the process.

However, it wasn't too long before it became obvious, even to John, that this plan was doomed from the start. Simple arithmetic should have told us that we were on a mission impossible. There were too many stops and many of them too far away to be achievable on our one journey per day plan.

Just for once we had to admit we were beaten. Quick as a flash I suggested that we still call the book Goin' Roon the Edge but instead of using the whole of the Scottish mainland we use the shoreline of the Caledonian Canal as the cut-off point. This would allow us to do the northern highlands and islands in a fourth book next year.

If you are lucky enough to have any more than three pints in you when an idea like that presents itself you grab it with both hands. Fortunately for the future of Scottish writing we were in an excellent position to accept this new concept. In fact we were in such a creative frame of mind that we even came up with a sub title for the book. It should be remembered that our original idea was to produce a three part series of books describing our travels around Scotland. The sub title arrived at the same time as our fifth pint. Some might call that coincidence. Anyway, we decided to call the book the third part of a four part trilogy.

John; So it's back to today's trip which started, as usual with me making up my pieces, which on this trip were made with chicken and English Mustard, which goes on everything I make. Kate and I had been down to Sainsburys the night before to get me some goodies, and I asked her to get Chicken Satay. Craig's Irene always gets him a packet which he shares with me, so I thought it would be nice to have some myself. When we got home, our son Ally, who lives just round the corner was in with the two kids, Sam and Evelyn. You wouldn't believe it, the two wee buggers almost ate the lot. Kate was pleased as it's better for them than sweeties. So there you go. I just hoped Craig believes my excuse for not having much Satay to share.

It was an early start. Kate set the alarm for 6.30am as I don't know how to do it. As usual I didn't need the alarm to wake me up. So with my pieces and what was left of the Satay packed in a Safeway poly bag, I wandered down to pick up Craig and catch the usual number 18 into Glasgow.

After a wee worry about the time the 18 was taking to get into Glasgow, we arrived with 10 minutes to spare, bought a paper and wandered over to stance 51 from where our Gold Bus, the G10, with the free tea and scones was leaving.

There were a few people waiting and as usual Craig was starting to worry about people jumping the queue. I don't know why he worried as there was going to be plenty of room on the bus. Our problem turned out to be an unusual one. The bus wasn't there, and didn't arrive till about 9.10am, 40 minutes late. This was a major worry as we had just under an hour before our connecting bus left Inverness.

This was all forgotten, by Craig anyway, when about half a dozen young boys, in their early 20s', started getting into the queue in front of us. It's bad enough when the oldies do this, they've an excuse. If they don't get on right away, they forget what they're doing and wander onto another bus.

Some of the boys, to be fair, were foreign. They may have been Italian, and as you know, Italians have no queuing gene in their bodies. This didn't help Craig who was livid and was trying to block them. It was embarrassing.

Peace was restored, and we had a great laugh when the driver told them, in a Highland accent that they were on the wrong bus. It made Craig's day, although he still says he's going to write to First Bus to complain about the lack of queue management in the Bus Station. I reckon Craig had threatened to write a letter of complaint to someone on each trip we have done so far. I'll have to keep an eye on him and his letters.

We settled in our comfy seats and enjoyed the great run up to Inverness. On the way we had our tea, scones and tablet, all free. On a serious note, it is really starting to worry me that I am looking forward to this type of thing-what has happened to my life? I am going to do a bucket list, and free tea and scones will not be on it.

After our lovely run up the A9, we arrived just in time to get our next bus, the City Link 919 to Fort Augustus, our next, and first proper port of call.

Goin' Roon the Edge

Craig; *A few days after all that deep thinking we set off for Inverness on our trip along the northern limit of our newly revised borders.*

As usual we began the day's trip in the middle of the night, or at least it felt that way. Waiting for the Gold Bus in Buchanan Street Bus Station we had plenty of time before the bus left the stance. Actually we had a hell of a lot of time before it left, most of it unplanned. There was no bus to be seen never mind boarded.

There wasn't much of a queue so I thought we could relax a bit. The problem was that quite a few of the oldies were sitting on the benches to wait for the bus. This meant that we couldn't go to the front of the queue and had to settle for hanging about at the back. We do have standards after all. The thing was this left a lot of empty space which could give the unscrupulous queue jumper a lot of room to manoeuvre. And that's exactly what happened.

When our bus eventually trundled into its stance, 30 minutes late, hordes of young hiking types started pushing into this space. John, as usual, didn't bother his arse about this state of affairs. So it was once again left to me to stop them all cheating their way on to the bus. To be honest I didn't do much of a job of it.

To listen to him you would think John had some sort of inside information on what was about to happen. There is no way he could possibly know that these young foreign queue jumpers were trying to get on the wrong bus.

Even without these would be interlopers the bus seemed fairly well filled by the time we managed to get on. Either I had miscounted the number of 'silver foxes' who had been sitting waiting or, and I think this is more likely, there were passengers already on the bus before it came in to the station. Just how they got on I have as yet failed to work out.

Still, we did manage to get two seats together so we settled down for the long trip up to Inverness. The trip itself was, as ever, very comfortable. While the scone, tea and tablet were delicious. I was particularly impressed by the wee girl serving them. She was nice and cheery and nothing was too much trouble for her. I was even offered extra sugar for my tea, an offer which I gladly accepted.

We were less than pleased to find out that because the bus was so late getting into the bus station then, for some unexplained reason, stayed there for another 20 minutes we would have no time in Inverness.

It wasn't just the fact that we might have fancied a beer in the town, which we did, but I had brought a book along to give to a pub owner we had met the last time we'd been there. We had promised to drop off a copy of our new book the next time we were passing. After all it did have the guy's picture in it along with our review of his pub.

To add insult to injury the pub was only fifty yards from the bus station. With a bit of a following wind I could have lobbed the thing to his front door.

John; Scottish people, especially older ones, are great characters. As we were getting on the bus, there was a fairly young French couple getting on and the girl was going on and on to her boyfriend, or husband, about something, no idea what, when the wee man behind them tapped the French bloke on the shoulder and said to him. 'This is why I'm no married pal'.

He turned round to me smiling so I said. 'You're dead right there wee man'. It's what keeps us happy on our travels, wee men like him.

It was a lovely run along Loch Ness, but trying to eat your pieces while keeping the camera ready for a Nessie shot is not easy. Craig was unhappy with the fact that we never got a pint in Inverness and with me for keeping saying, "Is that the monster?"

After a pleasant hour's journey, we arrived in Fort Augustus in time to catch the tail end of a wee shower. Fort Augustus is a lovely town, with the centerpiece being the six or seven locks which step up, or down, depending which way you're going, through the town. They are fantastic. We spent a while watching a gaggle of boats going up one or two of the locks before heading to our first watering hole of the day, *The Richmond House Hotel*. It was a nice wee bar and the bar lady was pleasant enough without putting herself out.

Locking up the boats.

At this stage of our trip I must tell you that for the foreseeable future, I am changing my drink from a pint of Best to a vodka and soda. There could be three reasons for this. One is that it is much cheaper, although Craig will not accept this in kitty matters. The second reason is that at my age, you need to kid yourself on that you're trying to lose weight, and vodka and soda has less calories, and alcohol I think, than a pint of Best. But the third and obviously only important one is that I have had an attack, my second one, of Gout. I'll tell you this, its agony, and the main way to avoid it is to stop drinking. This is also what Kate has advised me.

Me stopping drinking is not going to happen. So as a compromise I am going to stop drinking so often, change to vodka and soda, with possibly a glass of water between each drink, especially if Kate is with me, and lying about how many I've had when I'm away with Craig-I do this anyway, but Kate always knows exactly how many I've had.

Who could afford a lock in at The Lock Inn?

So back to the trip. After much slagging from Craig about me being a nancy boy, we left this pub and headed up and into *The Lock Inn*. This is a nice looking and atmospheric pub on the side of the locks. Years ago Kate and I, along with Sheila and her then partner Norrie (now called the bastard) hired a cabin cruiser for a long holiday weekend and after sailing up Loch Ness, which is not very nice, we had a laugh going up the locks at Fort Augustus. When we were out of the top one, we decided to wander back down and into the *Lock Inn,* which we had seen from our wee boat on the way up the locks. This was about 1.00pm, and the idea was to go in for an hour or so for a meal and a drink. To cut a long story short, we got into company and emerged from the pub about 10 at night. But we had a great day and it's a great pub.

I've got to admit that today the barman spent the time talking to a couple of boat people and ignored us altogether. Also the offhand way he treated a couple of foreign tourists looking for something to eat left a lot to be desired. Maybe he was new at the job or just Scottish.

So we left and headed down to the last pub in town, *The Bothy.* This is another nice looking and atmospheric bar, but again the barmaid, without doing anything wrong, showed no interest in talking to us or anybody else. Maybe it's not in the job description anymore. Fort Augustus is a great place to visit, mainly for the spectacle of the boats going up all the locks. It really is quite spectacular and worth a visit.

Craig; The next hour or so was a living nightmare for me personally. We were travelling down the side of Loch Ness to our revised first refreshment stop at Fort Augustus. John, for mysterious reason, thinks of himself as a bit of a comedian. I have my own idea which bit that is, but that's another story. Anyway, his routine that day was based entirely on his yelling out every five minutes "Is that the monster over there?" He would follow that up by saying "My mistake, it's only a wave."
I was ready for strangling him by the time we got to Fort Augustus. The passengers sitting nearest us would probably have helped me if I had. In between his hilarious routine John

149

tried to get some decent pictures of the great scenery we were passing through. I say tried but what I really mean is, failed miserably. He must have taken 25 or 30 shots of out of focus greenery. The monster could have been out on the side of the loch sun bathing for all he knew.

At one point the bus stopped to let off some tourists. It was raining at the time but this pair of geniuses stood there in the deluge, struggling to get into their waterproofs. We thought it was a wee bit odd that presumably sensible people would do this when there was a perfectly dry and empty bus shelter standing next to them. Very strange people these foreigners.

We resisted the charms of the scenic grandeur all around us in Fort Augustus and made straight for a place of refreshment. The Richmond House Hotel was not at all what I expected. I had expected Fort Augustus to be a real tourist trap so I thought we would find this place to be either an up-market lounge or a fake wine bar. It was neither. It was definitely meant for locals, and not very choosey locals at that.

The décor was a bit on the grubby side. Maybe well used would be a better description. They have either found a supply of beigey yellow paint or this bar hasn't been freshened up since well before the smoking ban came in. Perhaps the owners don't want to encourage passing trade. If that is the case then they're doing a bang up job of it. Actually I can see why they might want to do this. Unlike the hardy Scottish locals tourists don't tend to drink an awful lot. They expect high quality food and service and of course they expect the place to be dusted regularly. The locals on the other hand are more concerned with the volume and price of the booze. By the way it is very reasonably priced, for the Highlands.

The young barmaid was pleasant enough when she spoke to us. But it was all business. Then again she did have a glossy magazine which wasn't going to read itself.

Barmaid Rating ℞℞℞,

Goin' Roon the Edge

We didn't stay very long as John was keen to take in some of the scenery. Or, quite possibly it was his round. Whatever the reason we trudged up to the seven locks on the Caledonian Canal. Since he was forcing me to walk around the place I decided to get my revenge by telling him about the construction of the canal.

The man who built it did so for all the right reasons but it never really lived up to its potential. Thomas Telford (1757-1834) was one of Scotland's greatest engineers. He had built roads, bridges and canals all over Britain and Europe before he took on this huge project. It was meant to help Scotland's trade and provide employment for thousands of Highlanders. Unfortunately it did neither. Boats had begun to be built which were too big to fit through the canal's locks. Then the railways came along and further wasted things for the canal. It did however provide employment for about 19 years. But Highlanders being Highlanders much of the construction work was done by others, mainly Irishmen. The locals had a habit of wandering back to their crofts on a regular basis.

A friend once told me he had a pal who ran a small hotel in the Highlands which only employed foreigners. He claimed he couldn't use the local workforce. Apparently the young men thought hotel work was beneath them, while the young ladies of the town would work for a few months before getting themselves pregnant. So it would seem not a lot changes up there.

All of this in-depth history and scenery viewing took its toll on John. We had been walking along the side of the canal watching boats going up and down the locks. And now he looked in need of a good drink, then again he usually does. That's why we wandered into the wonderfully named 'Lock Inn', although, after we caught sight of the prices in the place, any thoughts of enjoying' a wee lock in' in this pub evaporated.

I would describe the décor as somewhere between a country tavern and a ski lodge.

While we were waiting for our drinks to come we had a chance to see the food menu. It made impressive reading. A fish supper was more than £11.00. That set the alarm bells ringing in my head. If only we had been a wee bit faster we could have legged it before the drinks arrived. I don't actually remember the exact price they charged for a pint. Maybe I was suffering from post-traumatic stress disorder, but it was certainly more than £3.50. I'll be lucky if I don't end up with a stutter.

It was comfortable in the 'Lock' but since my lottery numbers failed to appear at the weekend we couldn't afford another round of drinks.

Barman Rating 🍺🍺,

'The Bothy' looked like quite a nice wee place from the outside. And we were not disappointed by the inside either. To my mind the Bothy was a good compromise between the other two pubs in Fort Augustus. It was well decorated, but not over the top and seemed to appeal to both locals and tourists alike. Unfortunately it was also a bit on the expensive side, but I was getting used to this by that time.

The Bothy certainly looks a good age but I don't know how old it is. It can be hard to tell as sometimes newer pubs are decked out to look like traditional old ale houses.

Barman Rating 🍺🍺,

Just before we left for our bus to Fort William I decided a visit to the toilet was required. Unlike John I had been drinking manly pints all day. He's got it into his head that if he drinks vodka and soda the weight will just drop off him. I tried to explain to him that his plan would only make sense if he didn't drink gallons of it at every session, several times a week.

Anyway just finding the toilet was a bit of an adventure. It was upstairs and had obviously been a recent conversion. I can only think that the bulk of the renovation cash was spent elsewhere.

The entire toilet complex is located in the eaves of the building. I can testify that the sloping roof in the gents can be dangerous, if like me you fail to notice it straight away.

As I staggered backwards, suspecting a wee touch of concussion, I noticed a very curious addition to the usual sanitary fixtures and fittings. There was a full sized shower unit, minus the glass door, standing at the end of a row of sinks. I can only assume that it has just been left there since before the loft was converted into a public convenience.

If you ask me they are just asking for trouble leaving it there. It just takes one bus load of pint drinking Glasgow tourists, a bit of a queue at the urinals and we could be talking about an environmental catastrophe, especially if the plumbing has been disconnected.

John; It was soon time to wander over to the stop and catch our next bus, which was also a 919. It arrived spot on time and we had a lovely run down the other lochs to Fort William. This, like most of Scotland, is a beautiful area and with the bus pass to the fore, it's a great way to spend the day. Well done the numpties in the Scottish Parliament. You're great.

I've visited Fort William before and for a town situated in one of the most beautiful positions in Scotland, it is very disappointing in a visual sense. The town is separated from the water by a big road which means the front is sort of non-existent. I'm not saying it's anybody's fault, but the place is not much to look at, but should be.

However, that's a very small and unimportant fact when put beside the main issues we are trekking round Scotland looking into, the quality of service and friendliness, not just in pubs, but in tearooms, cafes and other places we never visit.

With that in mind we alighted (got off) the bus and wandered along the main street spying out pubs we could visit later when we had spent a couple of minutes sussing the town out. As I said, the front is not much to look at, but should be, but the main street is bright enough and the natives were all friendly. There were lots of young tourists about and everyone seemed happy. Fort William was growing on me.

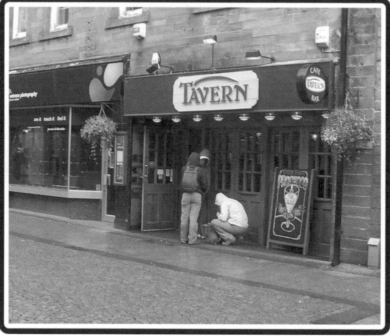

The lair of the Fort William village idiot.

The first pub we visited was called *The Tavern*. It was more of a restaurant type place, and apart from a discussion, or actually Craig having a discussion with a really weird bloke who continually asked us if we had been here or there, it was endless. The place was not bad, but only just. After about 20 minutes of this crazy guy asking where we had been, I told him where we were going, which was the hell out of here, and we left. We kept looking back to see if he was following us. He wasn't.

The next pub, *The Volunteer Arms,* was pretty drab, and again the barman, or bar boy, he was only about 18, showed no interest in conversation so we drank up and left.

Wandering further back up the main street, we despaired of finding a pub with anyone decent inside to talk to. That was until we spotted *Maryburgh Inn.* From the outside there is a sign in the street with the name on it and a set of dark stairs going down into the bowels of the earth. I doubt if any tourist in his right mind would want to go down the stairs to see what lived below. But we are not your usual tourists, and we were desperate to find a decent pub in Fort William.

And we found it. This is a great pub. The first thing you see when your eyes get accustomed to the light is a great big wishing well in the middle of the floor. This is a real wishing well and goes down hundreds of feet. The barman Geoff told us the history of the well and the bar in general.

Craig is really into history and things like that and was listening more to what Geoff was saying than I was, so I hope he will give you more details of the pub than I can. It was a great pub with great atmosphere and the bar maid Gillian, who bought two books, was great and a very interesting girl. When I asked her about the way she was dressed, which was very colourful and showey, she told me she practiced burlesque, just like my son Gregor's partner Michelle does. What a coincidence. The other girl Lillian, who helped out as a Scrubber, was also great.

Craig took photos of all the staff, and as you can see from the photo, they are all great looking and friendly people. We were really starting to enjoy ourselves.

As usual, we had found the best last, and all too soon it was time to leave, so we said a fond farewell to all the staff and customers, who were also great. We had a wee worry about two guys in the far corner. One of them was wearing a Celtic strip. Geoff will know who I mean.

Goin' Roon the Edge

Craig; *For as long as I can remember I have disliked Fort William. I don't know much about the place, I just don't like it. One thing I have noticed is that it always seems to be raining there. And today was no different.*

It is a straight walk from the bus station to the town centre, which is just as well really as we had no idea where we were supposed to be going. To be honest it's a bit bleak. This town centre would give Cumbernauld a run for its money in the ugly stakes. It seems to have been built facing away from the waters of Loch Linnhe so that when passing through the town on the coastal road the traveller gets a fine view of loading bays and skips.

We walked from one end of the centre to the other and we were not impressed. However there were a couple of likely looking pubs we thought deserved a visit. That just shows you about first impressions and why you shouldn't be guided by them.

Our first choice The Tavern was more of a café bar than a real pub. In fact it reminded me of the wee coffee bars which were popular back in the 60s.

Once again I managed to steal someone's seat at the bar, accidentally of course. I seem to be making a habit of that recently and it's a habit which can get you into all sorts of bother if you do it in the wrong place.

The former owner of the bar stool was very nice about it though and told me to just sit where I was. That was probably the last sensible thing he said while we were in the place. It can often be difficult to spot a nutter. They can be wiley creatures.

I'm usually quite good at spotting them and heading in the opposite direction, but on this occasion I slipped up. Within 60 seconds of starting to talk to him I realised that this guy was certifiable.

Fortunately, for me at least, John came back from the toilet and my new best friend latched on to him, leaving me to savour my pint of expensive slops in peace. I do remember one snatch of the conversation which sums up the surreal nature of the situation we found ourselves in.

The nutter-"Have you ever been to Sweden?"

John-"Yes I have."

The nutter-"How much are the meatballs."

I knocked back my pint in two gulps while John's vodka seemed to evaporate. We said our goodbyes and slowly backed out of The Tavern.

As the not so old saying goes, there are three things in life you should never turn your back on, a friend in need, a free drink and a nutter with easy access to sharp objects.

Barman Rating 🍺🍺,

Our next rest stop The Volunteer Arms, a much better choice in that there were no obviously homicidal maniacs lurking near the bar. Apart from that there was little else to cheer us in this place. There was nothing actually wrong with the pub, it was just a bit on the quiet side.

Barman Rating 🍺

I don't know which one of us spotted our next pub, 'The Maryburgh Inn'. The sign for the pub was obvious, but the pub wasn't. There just seemed to be a hole in the ground. On closer inspection we found a set of stairs leading into the bowels of the earth. Actually it was a basement really.

It was very dark and when I suggested to John that we go down and investigate what was down there he became very quiet. And that doesn't happen very often. Eventually I managed to persuade him to come with me and we descended into the darkness.

What we found was a great wee pub, once our eyes adjusted to the light, or lack of it. The first thing that struck me, and it very nearly did, was the four foot high, brick built, well which was in the middle of the floor. You don't see that too often so we stopped to take a look. It was about twelve feet deep and lit from the top. The bottom was completely covered with coins

157

and the whole thing was capped by a large piece of plate glass. A couple of the pub's customers were using it as a table, sitting their beer glasses on top of it. I couldn't do that. Imagine you had sipped a few beers and were to casually look over in the direction of the well, only to see beer glasses apparently floating in mid-air.

Geoff and Lilian (Barman and Scrubber)

We got talking to the barman, Geoff. He was a really good laugh and was interested in hearing about our books. Though apparently not interested enough to make buying one a prospect. Still, he was very friendly and introduced us to one of his staff, Lillian, who was standing at the end of the bar.
I didn't know where to look when he announced that she was the pub scrubber. That seemed to amuse the rest of his customers. I suspected that this was not the first time they had heard this little joke. She took it well though I have to say.

I felt that we should maybe try to find out the story behind the large, illuminated well in the middle of the bar. It really is the main feature of the place after all. That being said, we still managed to forget to take a picture of the dammed thing.

Anyway, I fully expected to hear some great historical tale about how the well had played an important role in Fort William's past, perhaps linked to the great '45 rising.

Instead Geoff told me that all he knew about it was that the building had been a ruin for many years and it was only when someone decided to build a pub there that they discovered the old dry well. Personally, if it had been mine I would have been a lot more creative about things. Bonnie Prince Charlie himself would have drawn water from my well for his tea every morning.

The barmaid, Gillian, came in and immediately started talking to us. That's the way it should be in pubs. A wee bit of patter works wonders for the character of a pub. She further ingratiated herself in our eyes by buying two of our books as a present for her dad. A very nice girl, is our Gillian, and a very lucky man is her dad. As it turns out she is very clever too. She is a graduate of Glasgow University.

Barstaff Rating R R R R R,

John; So with a renewed belief in mankind's ability to produce great pubs, we went back up the stairs and wandered back along the main street to the bus station. Before the bus arrived we nicked into the Morrison's next to it and got a couple of bags of crisps and stuff for the three hour journey home.

Our 916 City Link bus left sharp at 7.10pm and we had a great journey back down through Glen Coe and past Loch Lomond. We arrived back in Glasgow at about 10.15pm.

Believe it or not, we went straight down to the Central Station, stopping at the Blue Lagoon to get a couple of bags of chips with the watered down vinegar. I think we annoyed our fellow travellers on the train with the smell of the chips. They were great.

Irene was out babysitting and Kate was in her kip, so we got a taxi home. So ended a very busy and far travelled trip. Although we went a long way, the buses were great with toilets and everything, although you're still not allowed a wee bevy in them. I've still not written to the Scottish Parliament about this. I think I'll ask Craig to do it. He's the complainer.

Main Street, Fort William. If you think this is a midden you should see the back streets.

Craig; All to soon it was time to leave The Maryburgh Inn, but I would like to think that we will be back there for a pint some-day.

It was only after we got back upstairs and into the sunlight again that I remembered that after all our talk and questions about the wishing well we had forgotten to drop any money in

to it. In my defense I feel I should point out that John was in charge of the kitty money and doesn't part with cash easily
We caught our bus for the long haul back to Glasgow and I immediately noticed the difference, the vast difference between standard coaches and our beloved Gold coach. Never mind the comfort level of the seating it's the facilities which are the real eye opener.
Until now I have resisted the dubious pleasure of using the WC on standard coaches. The toilet on the Gold coach could pass muster in any small five star hotel room. However I was obliged to use the toilet on the Fort William to Glasgow bus and I would have to say it would not be out of place in the poorer quarter of a Bolivian shanty town.
Maybe from now on I will have to follow John's example and take up Nancy boy drinking.
Apart from the trauma caused by having to use this cludgie from hell, as we bounced along the A82, the journey home passed without incident.

John; *My Spends for the day;*
Bus Fares;   £0.00
Train fares;   £0.80 (back from Glasgow to EK)
Chips;   £1.95 (how's that for memory)
Snacks;   £3.00 (crisps and papers etc)
Drink;   £24.00
Total;   **£29.75 (cheap day)**

If you don't drink, a fiver would cover a great day out and you would waken up feeling great. You would be able to bore your friends about your day in the Highlands. But remember, hangovers go away, friends don't like being bored.

A Fairlie nice day oot

*(Travelling up the Ayrshire coast,
Past the scenery we like the most)*

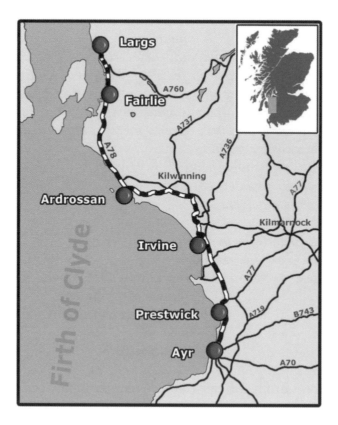

Ayr-Prestwick-Ardrossan-Fairlie-Largs

Goin' Roon the Edge

John; To the eagle eyed among our readers, or ones sober enough to remember what happened more than a few days ago, part of this trip was covered in our last best seller, but since this is 'Goin' Roon the Edge', we felt we must re-trace some of the same area. So we could say we went round the edge, if that makes sense, but with one major difference. We would visit different towns and pubs therein. How's that for a shocker.

Ayr to Largs has some lovely bits, and some howlers. I am not going to tell you which is which as I do not want to offend the residents of Kilwinning and Ardrossan. Only kidding you guys!

This was an easy trip to organize. Once we get to Ayr, every bus to take us from place to place is the 585 which trundles along the coast from Ayr to Greenock every hour or so, a bit of timetable information for you there.

For a change it was not an early start, I think you all know that we work backwards. The pubs open at 11.00am, so we leave in enough time to be at our first port of call in time for the day's most important event. The 10.01am X16 from East Kilbride filled the bill perfectly for this event, opening time. This also meant that I would have enough time in the morning to make my pieces, so freshness would be guaranteed and the Corned Beef would still be firm, not to mention the sharpness of the English Mustard, which does lose its edge after a while out of the jar.

So after a long lie, I got ready, made the pieces, with a couple of extras slipped into the poly bag, and wandered down to get Craig. As usual, he had the big haversack ready, which is always a good sign as it is full of goodies which he shares with me. He has little option as I offer to carry the haversack.

It was a miserable morning, dull and wet, more like an Autumn morning, which it actually was, so instead of walking the two stops to the bus station, we did the dry thing and got a number 18 down to the bus station.

163

Walking would have been no problem for me as I had a new, £18 umbrella with me. Obviously I would never spend that sort of money on anything other than drink, but someone had given me a £20 voucher for John Lewis for my birthday, and the only thing in the shop I could buy with that sort of money was an umbrella. I'm certain I will lose it on some trip. I've lost a few £1 ones in previous trips.

We were in plenty of time for the X16, so I got some money out of the hole in the wall and bought a paper. As usual I bought the Daily Mail to see if they were mentioning any of my ultra-right wing policy ideas, and Craig got his left wing rag, The Daily Record.

I have noticed recently that I am doing daft things, even when sober. I kid myself on that it is just old age, but Craig says it is something more sinister. The other day I was coming away from the self-service tills in our local Sainsbury's and had a 20 pence change and the receipt in my hand. Instead of throwing the receipt into the bin, I threw the 20 pence into it.

The reason I mention this is that something similar happened on the X16. We were about to settle into our seats when I realized I had lost my mobile. To cut a long, and embarrassing story short, I was on my hands and knees on the bus when it fell out of my shirt pocket. It's definitely getting worse. I've asked Craig not to slag me off about this in his version of today's events.

Pretending nothing had happened, we settled down to a fairly miserable run down to Ayr. It rained the whole way and the windows were steamed up. Luckily we haven't had many days like this, and as we know this area very well, we can describe the scenic grandeur without seeing it.

Craig; *The best thing about this trip was the fact that it is a fairly local journey and that means of course that we could set off at a reasonable time. Most of our recent journeys have begun at the crack of dawn.*

The X16 is a great bus service; we have used it a few times before and have been very impressed with it. Funny how ideas change!

I was looking for our bus coming into the station in EK, but still managed to miss it approaching. The trouble was I was looking for a nice sleek, double decker and what was ambling towards us was neither nice, nor sleek. It was a shabby old single decker. Just like the one that had nearly ruined my back on one of our trips last year. Somewhere, in a small 3rd world country, the local transport company is missing a bus. I know where it is. Now I'm all for keeping costs down, but not fitting shock absorbers seems like a false economy to me.

I also think that someone, out to make a fast buck, has slipped some extra seats into this bus. There was hardly any room to move, I nearly did myself an injury trying to get my jacket off.

What a surprise! We got in here no problem.

John; Getting off the bus the stop before the bus station, we crossed the river Ayr, and I look a lovely picture from the bridge. The rain was off and the day was clearing. Not that it mattered too much as we were heading for the dryness of our first pub of the day, which turned out to be *The Campbeltown Bar*. It was a traditional man's bar, and had a good few old men in it.

There were about six of them sitting round a table, and the patter was typical of what men talk about when together in a pub, a load of rubbish. I overheard them talking about the Black Forest and this led to Black Forest Gateau. It was absolute rubbish, I felt right at home and would have joined them if there had been room. The bar itself was fairly depressing and the barman didn't give us the time of day, so after downing our drinks, we wandered out and round the corner to a nice looking pub called *The Black Bull*.

The first thing I noticed in the pub was a sign with the opening hours which showed that the pub opened at 10am, and not 11am as is the normal inland. Craig told me that it is because of the local fishing industry. Seemingly the boats come in early in the morning and the fishermen can then have a pint. Looking down to the river, the fishing industry was not as big as it once might have been, although I did see a wee boy with a fishing rod in his hand.

The barmaid told us that most of the pubs in Ayr open at ten. She said it was great for the tourists down for the weekend, 'they just fall out of bed and into the pubs'. I was starting to like Ayr. This was a great wee bar and we could have stayed longer if not for our rigid timetable. But this is the one bar out of the two that is worth a visit.

Kate and I were in Ayr about a week or so earlier delivering some books to the Waterstones store in the High Street. As we were walking up the street we heard a voice shouting, 'away back to Rothesay'. We looked round and there was big Dougie, a friend, and very funny guy from Rothesay, who was over on a shopping trip for the day with the wife, who was in some shop or other.

When we told Dougie that we were delivering books that I had written, he right away told us that he had been working on a book since he retired two years ago. He said so far he had coloured in the first two pages! What a laugh!

Craig; Once again we had managed to find the only seat on the bus with a working heater. And it was working at full blast. In short, it wasn't a good trip down to Ayr. The only amusing thing to happen on our journey was when John went into his comedy routine. It was like watching Mr. Bean in 3D.

He had lost his phone; the big problem was his jacket has more pockets than a couple of snooker tables. Every time we go on a trip he discovers yet another hidden pocket. He stood up and starting searching his pockets for the phone. When he didn't find it he started all over again. This went on for about five minutes getting faster and faster. Anybody looking round might have thought he was beating out flames. Some old women came over to see if they could help him. It was only when he had bent over to look under the seat that his phone popped out of his top pocket. I didn't know whether to laugh or give him a hard slap. I chose to laugh.

Passing through Prestwick we each chose a side of the bus to look out of hoping to spy some decent pubs for later on. Once in Ayr we made for the 'Campbeltown Bar'. I have often seen this pub but only in the passing. This time we were going in. It's really tempting fate for us to have anything to do with Campbeltown. We have a bit of history with the town of that name, but we were feeling lucky.

Inside the pub could be said to be a wee bit on the drab side. There's absolutely nothing wrong with that of course. It's an old man's pub after all, that being said a wee lick of paint and the odd bit of carpentry wouldn't go amiss. There may well be a perfectly good reason to have a hole in the bar, but if not, maybe nailing a bit of wood over it would save others from catching their jacket sleeve on it. Despite the large chunk of nothing where a part of the bar should be I still liked it. It was like stepping back in time. The height of the bar really impressed me. You don't see many oxter high bars anymore. It really reminded me of my apprenticeship at the bar. Back then nothing about pubs was comfortable. There was no padding on seats, no bar stools and no cheery barman. They always seemed to be either depressed or angry.

At least this was the way I remember it anyway. The bars were very tall which meant you were always looking up at the bar staff. My only other memory of those days was the fact that there was very little colour about pubs. Everything was sepia. Apart from the flat screened tellies tuned as ever to the horse racing channel, the 'Campbeltown' looked like the old pubs in the early 70s. Some old guys were playing some sort of game at a table, We never found out what it was exactly that they were playing. Actually I didn't really want to catch their eye as it seemed they were in the mood to slag everyone within earshot. One pint was enough for us and we moved on.

Barman Rating 🍺🍺🍺,

Our next port of call was 'The Black Bull' and we immediately decided it was a contender for our pub of the day award, if only we did in fact have such an award to present. It was a bit on the minimalistic side in décor, but this was a man's pub so that was just fine. The place was almost empty which to be honest wasn't really a surprise given it was only 11.45am.

We got talking to the barmaid, who was very nice and cheery. John mentioned something about the pub not being very busy. He really is a master of the obvious sometimes. That was when the barmaid surprised us both. She said that if we had come in an hour earlier we would have seen that the place was jumping. John did a quick mental calculation and, five minutes later announced that meant the pub must have been open before eleven o'clock. There was almost a tear in his eye by this time as he has always wanted to find an early opening pub. I had told him that some of the pubs down by the harbour used to open at six in the morning for the men off the fishing boats. I don't think he believed me, but here we were in a pub which opened at 10 in the morning. It was almost a spiritual experience for him and indeed he wandered around for the rest of the day with a serene smile on his face. Of course it could simply have been trapped wind, it's hard to tell.

We left the pub with John promising to return one day very soon, presumably very early in the morning.

Barmaid Rating ℞℞℞℞

John; But back to today's trip, Craig and I left the bar and made our way along to the nearest bus stop and got on a number two, not a 585 as planned. There are hundreds of buses going along the main street from Ayr to Prestwick, our next port of call.

As the bus went along and into Prestwick, I remembered a story a friend of mine, Graeme told me about Old Prestwick Golf Club (I think it might be Royal as well, I don't know). Anyway, Prestwick is one of the Scotland's oldest, and one of the most traditional golf clubs in the world.

So this day, about 20 or so years ago, Graeme's dad was playing (with an American friend) over the ancient links. The plan was that the friend's wife would come and pick them up after the round. Arriving before they were finished their round, the lady wandered into the clubhouse, only to be thrown out as ladies were not allowed in the clubhouse, unless they are waitresses. She was none too chuffed, but didn't want to create a fuss in a foreign country, so she went back to her car, which was in the car park to nurse her wrath and wait for the men. The secretary of the club, who was watching, came out and over to the car and told her to get out of the car park as women were not allowed there either. Why can't we have rules like that nowadays? This is a true story by the way!

Again, back to today, like Ayr, and Troon for that matter, Prestwick has a big beach which on any nice sunny day of the year is brilliant, but on days like today is very depressing, but is great if you like fresh air, walking the dog, jogging, or just getting soaked. Needless to say we headed into a wee bar called *Smugglers*. This is a nice bar and the lady serving was very pleasant and we had an enjoyable chat and a nice pint, or vodka and soda in my case, still trying to lose weight and avoid the Gout.

While we were in the bar, we discovered that many of the pubs in Prestwick open at 9am in the morning. Before you ask, there is definitely no fishing industry in the town. Craig was starting to wish he had never left Ayrshire.

Wanting to see more of the town, we wandered about a bit. Prestwick is a really nice wee town and well worth a visit, using the bus pass of course. But a warning to the ladies, don't go near the golf club.

Before leaving, we went into *The Red Lion*. Now there is nothing wrong with this bar if you have kids or are planning to eat. But it is not a man's bar and reminded us of a Wetherspoon's type of place. Nothing wrong with that if that's what you like, but not for us.

Craig; On our journey to Prestwick we passed a pub I thought I recognized from years ago. On the strength of that memory we walked back to it as soon as we got off the bus. Actually I didn't remember it being called 'The Smugglers' and once inside I didn't remember the place at all. There is every chance this wasn't the pub I thought it was.

One thing I did notice about it was that it was empty. That's never a good sign at one o'clock in the afternoon. Going against the grain, I was on the point of suggesting to John that we forget about having a pint in the place and move on, when the barmaid eventually showed up. Things then got a bit better and we enjoyed the rest of our stay.

The beer was a bit on the expensive side which I thought was a bit ironic for a pub called 'The Smugglers'. While we were sipping our pricey brews, the barmaid was using a funnel to fill up one of those giant bottles of vodka which sit on the gantry. She saw us looking and said that it gets busy later on Fridays. I was glad we were not going to be there later.

Barmaid Rating

We made our way up the road to 'The Red Lion' after that. I had been into this pub many years ago and had fond memories of the pub, which is a bit of a pity because it had all changed, and not for the better. Instead of a traditional country pub, it had changed into one of those horrible pub chain places, everyone looking like each other. We had no contact with the bar staff other than when we ordered our drinks. They were probably far too busy organizing their social lives. That was bad enough, but there was a juke box playing some of the worst music I've heard in years and the place was jumping, quite literally, with weans. It was time to go.

Bar staff Rating,

John; We had 10 minutes to wait for our next bus, so as it was dry and we were looking over lovely gardens, we decided to sit on the wall and have our pieces. I had Corned Beef with English Mustard. This is my normal, but not exclusive choice of fillings, and today I had Beetroot on the Corned Beef. This can be a dodgy combination as if the beetroot is wet, it seeps through the bread, but everything was ok. I told Craig I had licked the Beetroot dry. Amazingly, this sort of information puts him off his pieces, I love it.

Full up, we got on the 585 and both slept some of the way to our next destination. Ardrossan is one of these places that you do not want to go to, but if we missed out all the dodgy places on the Scottish coast, the book would not be very thick.

The main thing most people know about Ardrossan, is that the ferry to Arran leaves from here. It comes back as well.

The main street looked pretty grim, and the first pub we ventured into, *Charlie's Bar,* fitted the street perfectly. We managed to finish our drinks without making eye contact with anyone and left quietly. It was that sort of place.

Fortunately, round the corner in a back street was a wee bar called *Castlehill Vaults.* This was a nice bar and the barmaid, and locals in it were normal looking and we felt at home there. The drink was fine and prices were reasonable, but like many bar staff in Scotland, the barmaid kept to herself. Now there is nothing wrong with keeping to yourself, but a bit of interaction with other people can be a great thing, especially if the customer is on his or her own.

Our wee Hideaway from the towns Jakies.

While we were waiting for our next 585 to get us out of Ardrossan, there was a wedding across the road, and the bride and guests were, as is normal in Scotland, dressed up. I think this is a Scottish tradition. Once, Kate and I were at a wedding down south and many of the guests seemed to be wearing their normal clothes. This is seemingly normal in the South of England. Maybe our normal clothes are so bad we need to buy new stuff for a wedding. I don't know.

Craig; Ardrossan sees an awful lot of tourists every year. Thankfully the clever ones keep on moving through. The Arran ferry leaves from the town every two hours or so. It's not a place most people would consider stopping in, unless they are looking for trouble or are pub reviewing bus travellers.

Actually I was surprised to find any pubs open in the town. I imagined that the only thing open in that area was the ferry port. Eventually we found a pub and gratefully entered. Talk about rough. But as they say beggars can't be choosers. 'Charlies Bar' is not for the faint hearted. There was a bit of a smell about the place. I'm not sure if it was death or stale beer. We were hoping it was the beer. John was getting a bit agitated so we didn't hang around too long.

Barman Rating 🍺🍺,

Down the road and up a wee lane we found a much better place, 'The Castlehill Vaults'. It was much quieter so we both relaxed a bit. The customers seemed to have formed three distinct groupings. There were half a dozen younger men sitting at a table laughing and joking. At the bar, what I would describe as a group of middle aged men were chatting away happily. The only other occupied table had four older men sitting at it. They were making more noise than the other two groups put together.

It struck me that these other two groups were just biding their time until they progressed to the old boy's table, a bit like apprentices serving their time. I don't know which table John and I would be invited to join if we became regulars.

173

We enjoyed our beers which were reasonably priced then left to catch our next bus.

Barman Rating R R R,

John; The bus arrived, and with a sigh of relief, we left Ardrossan behind and the bus took us along the lovely coast road on its way to Fairlie, our next destination. On the way, the bus takes a detour up and through West Kilbride. Craig complained as usual. He thinks people who live in wee places off the main road should be made to walk to the main road to catch the bus. What a moan he is.

Fairlie is a small town, or village, on the banks of the Clyde overlooking The Great Cumbrae, or it used to before a giant coal terminal was built blocking any view the locals may have had from their seafront houses. What a bummer that must have been.

Craig had checked Google and knew there was a nice wee bar called *The Village Inn.* So we got off the bus and found the Inn without any bother. Before going in we went down to the front to admire the view of the huge terminal with The Cumbrae somewhere in the background. I suppose you can't stop progress, but like wind farms, why does progress have to be so ugly.

The Inn itself was very nice, in an up market sort of way. There are about three very big marinas in the area, so I suppose they need to offer the Arran Sweater brigade somewhere to spend their money is important to the owners, and so it should be. I'm not complaining.

We had a nice time in the bar and a good chat with Bob, a local who gave us all the background to what is going on in the area. A thing I thought was interesting is that all the coal that arrives comes from South America. It makes me, and Arthur Scargill I suppose, wonder why we couldn't have made a go of continuing mining in this country, but there you are.

Again, the bar staff were very nice without trying to engage us in any conversation. At one stage I had one of our books out, but had no luck selling one. I thought that with all the money about a book was bound to go, but no interest was shown.
We had a couple of drinks before saying goodbye to Bob and wandering up to the main street and catching our last 585 of the day on the five minute run along the coast into Largs.

A Fairlie good place to stop for a drink.

Craig; When we got off the bus in Fairlie, I knew exactly where we had to go to find our next refreshment stop. 'The Village Inn' is a very nice little place, in fact it's actually not that wee. I had used my computer to find this place and was very chuffed that things had worked out the way they did. John was very impressed with my computing skills. What he didn't know was that when I had looked at 'The Village Inn' on Google Street View, the place looked shut. There were heavy metal shutters on the doors and windows. Had it been closed I think John would have cracked up.

We talked to a few of the locals and had a laugh at things in general. I managed to have a word with the barman, he might have been the owner but I couldn't swear to it as it had been a very long day. Anyway I told him about checking the place out on Google and he got a bit animated. It seems that the pub has lost a fair bit of trade because the pictures on line are out of date.

The pub was closed for quite a long time before being bought by the present owners. Unfortunately, Google have not updated their pictures. Apparently the owners have tried to have it taken down but so far nothing has been done. So much for technology that's what I say.

Barman Rating 🍺🍺🍺,

John; Now we have covered Largs already and the reason for finishing there is that the terminus for the Glasgow train is there. But Largs is a great place and worth a few visits.

We were not in a great hurry, so we got off the bus at the station, got our tickets to EK and knew we had well over an hour before our planned train, so we headed to a pub we had both seen in previous trips, but had never visited. So we set out from the station to find it.

After wandering across the main street and round a few corners we found it. It is called *The Royal Oak Bar* and it is a great, and very atmospheric bar. We had a great time in it and had a couple of drinks. The locals were a great crowd, but one guy in particular never shut up. He was worse than me, if that's possible. He had an English accent, but claimed he was from Northern Ireland. He gave us his life story, but he never stopped talking so you never knew when his life story finished and by then you just wanted to shoot yourself, or him. I could see Craig was getting irritated. He is easily upset, so I suggested we should leave and get the train home.

We actually had plenty of time, so we managed to call in at a Fish and Chip shop for a bag of chips. They were magic.

Goin' Roon the Edge

Craig; *Instead of simply getting the train from Largs as soon as we got there, we decided to check out a pub we had seen in Largs but never actually had a drink in. 'The Royal Oak Bar' is on a back street and is a very good looking pub, in fact it is probably one of the best kept looking bars in the town. Inside we almost immediately got chatting with a couple of the pub regulars. All seemed to be going well until one of them started telling us absolutely everything he had ever learned in his entire lifetime. I hate one sided conversations, especially when the person conversing is a genuine loony. Luckily for me I have the ability to tune out this kind of nonsense. It is a skill I have developed over many years drinking in some of the rougher pubs in Ayrshire.*

The only drawback to having this gift is that sometimes you can miss something important. Not that something important ever came out of the mouth of this pub pest. Out of the corner of my eye I could see some of the locals sneaking out of the side door. They had probably been waiting all afternoon for some poor unsuspecting big softy to come in and take up this guy's attention. We put up with his nonsense for as long as we could but eventually we could stand it no longer, so we left.

Barman Rating 🍺🍺🍺🍺

John; As usual, we slept most of the way home and arrived in Glasgow Central refreshed. It was Friday night, and only about 8 o'clock, so we had to have a couple of pints somewhere. I had not been in Glasgow this late on a Friday for years and was amazed at how busy, and loud everywhere was. We were thinking about going into *The Two Headed Man* for a quick one, but the noise was ridiculous, so we crossed Hope Street and went round the corner and into *The Rodreck Doo,* at least I did. Craig's normal gait is walking with his head down, and desperate for the toilet as he was, didn't notice that he had gone into the nightclub entrance next door. He was stopped by the bouncer and told it cost £6 to get in. I was wondering where he had got to and had the round up by the time he appeared, and then disappeared, to the free toilet.

Our drink was ruined, for Craig anyway, by England scoring three quick goals in a world cup qualifying match that was being shown on a big telly screen you couldn't avoid seeing, so we finished our drinks and wandered back across Hope Street and round to *The Horse Shoe Bar,* our regular safe haven in Glasgow. There are tellies in there as well, but we stood where Craig did not have to watch the auld enemy enjoying themselves. No idea how the game ended.

An enjoyable drink later, we headed back to The Central Station and got our train home. As Craig was about to text Irene our details for a pickup, she phoned Craig, who, unlike me was fairly well on, and tried to get me to answer the phone. What a coward he is. Needless to say I'm a bigger coward and he had to talk to Irene, who, bless her, still came and picked us up and took us home.

We had a great day out on the Clyde Coast but were glad to be home. This is an easy trip for anyone to organize, and on a good day would be a great day out.

Craig; *Today's trip has been more or less a local trip for me and therefore we hadn't spent a lot of time on the buses. This meant we had a bit of extra time on our hands so we set about using this time checking out different pubs in Glasgow before heading back up to East Kilbride. I had suggested to John that we try out 'The Two Heided Man' in Hope Street. At least that's what I told him we were going to do.*

I had been in this establishment before and I wanted to see if John's reaction would be the same as mine.

'The Two Heided Man' is the name of a Matt McGinn song and as a bit of a fan I thought I would pay a visit to the pub named after one of his better known works. I had imagined that the pub would be some kind of tribute to his memory. What it turned out to be was a complete midden. It was well ahead in

178

the running to be the worst pub it has ever been my misfortune to have a drink in. Most places have at least one saving grace. This one managed to have absolutely nothing going for it. John, to his credit, spotted it for what it was from across the road, so we didn't bother going in.

Round in Cadogan Street we had a wee bit of a mix up. I took my eyes off John for just a second and he was gone. It's like looking after a wean, so it is. I assumed he was suffering a bladder emergency and had nipped into the nearest pub. That was a mistake and I have had to listen to him going on about it ever since. A quick drink in 'The Roderick Dhu' then a slow one in the 'Horseshoe' rounded off the day for us.

John; *My spends for the day;*

Bus Fares;   £0.00
Train Fares;   £3.70 (Largs to EK)
Can't get bus back to Glasgow as no lavies aboard)
Food;   £1.70 *(Chips in Largs)*
Drink;   £36.00
Total;   **£41.40**

I wish I had never started doing this as today looks really bad, but remember, I sometimes buy a soda water and lime with my vodka and soda-that's my excuse anyway.

The two old chappies
O' Lower Largo

*(Leven Lower Largo on the road to Pittenweem,
It Elie is nae distance, twelve miles it would seem)*

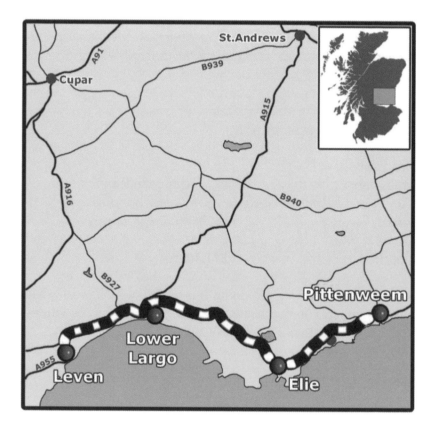

*Leven-Lower Largo-Elie-
St. Monans-Pittenweem*

Goin' Roon the Edge

John; Even for West of Scotland people like Craig and I, the names of the places we planned to visit just run off the tongue. Most people from the West have visited the East Neuk of Fife for a holiday when they were young. It was a favourite for families, Boy's Brigade and Scout camps. I would say this area is Glasgow's equivalent of Dunoon, Rothesay, Largs and Millport.

Travelling along the coast from Kirkcaldy to St. Andrews, there are so many well-known wee places, we knew that we could not possibly do it all in one day, so we planned two - genius. An overnight break halfway along would have been the answer, but the ladies imagined we would enjoy ourselves too much doing this. They claim we are drunk enough when we get home without an overnight to add to our enjoyment. Of course, this meant another early start, but at our age you don't sleep well anyway, so that argument fell on deaf ears.

I was really looking forward to this trip, even if the forecast was a bit ropey. We were coming to the middle of September after all. So it was up at 7.00am, a quick shower and breakfast, pack pieces I had made the night before and out the door for 7.40am to pick up Craig. A piece of culinary information about my pieces (are piece and pieces spelt the same, I've no idea), I went for chicken again. Not the cheapest I could have bought in my local Sainsbury's, but Bernard Matthews make. I was amazed he made them as I always thought Turkeys were all he did. However I think I am slowly going away from the Corned Beef. I think it is because of Craig's continuing hatred of the Argies getting through to me. Where was I, oh yes, the journey. We got the No. 18 as usual. I am really bored with this bus as it is the one we start almost all journeys with. Think I'll ask Kate if she fancies a move to a wee flat near Buchanan Street Bus Station. Just think of all the time that could be saved if you lived there.

Goin' Roon the Edge

Craig; I had been looking forward to this trip up the East Coast. Who wouldn't want to visit a place called Lower Largo? It just sounds like the kind of place we would find interesting. In fact I was so convinced we were going to have a great time I forgot to check out the availability of pubs in that wee town.

Our bus was approaching Leven before it dawned on me that I had failed in my duty to search for the most important aspect of any of our travels, licenced premises. That rather took the shine off the day. Each of our target destinations was a worry for me after that. It's bad enough when I claim to have seen a nice village pub only to find out that it's been closed for a couple of years. Bloody Google! I still remember the cold feeling in the pit of my stomach, not to mention John's cold staring eyes, when we discovered both of the village pubs were shut on our visit to Creetown in Galloway.

The day started like many other trip days, with me wishing we weren't going away. I think it's my inbuilt laziness. Once I'm up and around for half an hour or so, had a large mug of tea and watched the news headlines, I'm raring to go. Well as near raring to go as I ever get these days. With a little encouragement and a lot of organizing from Irene I was ready when John arrived, dead on time as usual, at my door-what a man.

John; As usual we read the free paper on the bus and ignored the Jakies and weird people going into the city centre for God knows what reason.

As usual, time was tight and I started to worry when Craig told me that George Square was closed from 6.00am this morning because there was going to be a parade of Scotland's Olympic Champions at 4.00pm this afternoon. Why the square has to be closed all day to allow about a dozen sportsmen and women to do a parade is beyond me; another thing to moan about.

This usually meant that the bus went right along past George Square and up West Nile Street, adding about 10 minutes to the

182

journey. Ten minutes we didn't have. The problem was solved when an inspector got on the bus and told us we would go right up High Street and along Cathedral Street to the bus station. This means nothing to non-Glasgow readers, but I thought I'd tell you all anyway. So this route, linked to the driver taking a wee back street short cut meant that we arrived in plenty of time for our bus to Leven. Reckon the driver must have been a Glasgow man, although, come to think of it, he seemed pleasant enough!

The X26 Glasgow to St. Andrews bus was ours and it was almost empty when it left the bus station.

Although the weather was miserable in Glasgow, as soon as we passed Cumbernauld, which you really want to do, it cleared up and the sun came out and stayed out all day in the East of Scotland. The journey was very enjoyable and soon we were in Leven Bus Station.

Craig; As usual we grabbed a couple of copies of the Metro to read on the bus down to Glasgow. Also as usual we had managed to grab a couple of copies each. It was very early you must remember.

I like to read on this bus as it helps me avoid eye contact with my fellow travellers. It's not that I dislike them, not all of them anyway, it's just too early in the morning. People are still half asleep. They stare into space, they stare at the roof and unfortunately the stare at each other. It's really hard to tell if someone is staring at you or if they are just still half asleep, hence the reading of the papers.

Most people will have worked out by now that I'm a very easy going guy who doesn't get annoyed easily. But some things really get to me. One of the most annoying things about using public transport is that some of the public are utterly selfish morons, especially the ones who listen to personal stereos. I use this term to include i-phones, i-pods and any other i's they come up with. The point is they are anything but personal.

Goin' Roon the Edge

While all my other faculties are in steep decline, my hearing remains exceptional. This should be a good thing, but on buses it can be a curse. The tinny screeching coming from all these devices drives me mad. I live in hope that some clever soul will invent a machine which knocks out these awful music players. Until then I have to control the urge to snip their headphone wires.

The situation might be a little easier to bear if these people would turn the volume down to merely deafening. Actually listing to good music might also help. One final thought occurs to me, and that is I think we are raising an entire generation of people who will be stone deaf by the time they're 40.

John; We had a wander down to the front and round the town. Leven doesn't have the picturesque small harbour that most of the East Neuk towns have and the place reminded me of a smaller, but slightly nicer version of Kircaldy. I would imagine Leven is a starting off point for tourists visiting the area.

Ye Old Crown Inn was our choice of pub for our first drink of the day, and it was a very pleasant, but not exceptional place. The barmaid was pleasant enough but did not try to make any kind of conversation with us. She could probably see we would be trouble and bore the backside off her.

I have no idea how our sing song started. I think Craig is getting as daft as me. As we were discussing the leaving of Leven, I thought about the famous song, The Leaving of Liverpool. In the time it takes to swing a cat, Craig burst into;

It's not the leaving of Leven that greaves me so
But the journey up to Lower Largooo

I put it down to the change of life, remember, he was sober. Our next bus was supposed to be the 12.30pm X26 which would take us to Upper Largo and we would then walk down to Lower Largo, our next port of call, but being experienced travellers, we picked up a local bus timetable and found that the 12.15pm number 95 would take us right down into Lower Largo. So on we got and enjoyed the 10 minute run along the east coast and down into Lower Largo. The sun was out and the bus dropped us off right at the Harbour which is at the mouth of the river (don't know the name). There is an old stone viaduct there which took the trains over the river, when there were trains. The place looked beautiful and moved Craig to take plenty of photos instead of making a bee line to the nearest pub.

We're right on track with the Railway Inn.

We had a wander around the town which brought back memories of two holidays I had there when I was young. The memories were pretty vague, but they were there, somewhere. Lower Largo is famous for the Robinson Crusoe story, which I hope Craig will fill you in with in his version of today's trip He is the better read one of us, in fact the only one of us who has read anything except The Mail.

Craig; Our bus to Leven was quite comfortable. Actually it was so comfortable I slept most of the way there. I quite liked what little we saw of Leven. We didn't have very much time to spend in the town but it seemed to be a busy well laid out town centre. The Crown was to be our only refreshment stop in Leven and I have to say it wouldn't suit me as a local. It was very early so the place wasn't very busy. We were served quickly and fairly cheerfully but the barmaid didn't stop to chat.

Maggie pulling the pints in Lower Largo.

The bar itself was very bright and quite comfortable. I did like the fact that the bar was fully carpeted but wondered what the pub cleaner thought of that. On a rainy day I would imagine it would be manky with people trailing in and out on their way to the bookies. It's definitely a racing pub, and that is reason enough for me to want to go elsewhere. The four flat screen tellies were split between a music channel and the racing one. Other clues to the notion that we were standing in a sporting man's pub were the framed prints of various nags and jockeys looking like winners and a framed jockey's shirt which I assume came from a famous local celebrity. I was overwhelmed with apathy.

Barmaid Rating; ⬛⬛

John; There were two places to wet the whistle (no idea what whistle means) at the Harbour, *The Crusoe Hotel* and the *Railway Inn*. We reckoned we would be visiting both, but we thought the *Inn* looked the best bet, and we were right.

The bar was great, the barmaid Maggie was fantastic and the two regulars at the end of the bar, Bill and Alasdair were great company. Both were retired and I think Alasdair said he was in his 90s'. I'm sure that's what he said, but he was as fit and active as I am, although that's maybe not saying much.

They filled us in on the history of the place and themselves, and the different things to do in the dark nights in Largo. One of the more interesting pastimes used to take place on some Friday nights. The older locals played strip dominoes. The thought put me right off my drink, for a minute. But you couldn't help yourself asking how it worked, and if one of the old guys said he was chappin, would some old woman get out the Sudocrem, and what would a double blank mean you had to take off? The mind boggles. I don't know if Craig heard the answer, but I started talking to Maggie to avoid hearing. They were having a great laugh anyway.

We were getting to the stage of buying each other drinks and then Bill gave me a present of a Plaque depicting a golfer. He makes them himself and I was delighted with his generous gift.

Bill and Alasdair - strip domino champions of Lower Largo.

I was so overcome with emulsion that I presented Bill and Alasdair with a copy of each of our books. That's £16 we'll never see again. You can be so generous when you've had a few.

We had already missed the planned bus, but were at the stage that we didn't care. I asked Craig if he wanted to go over and check out the *Crusoe Hotel. H*e said he didn't. So I, being the more sober one and believing that our readers need to know about all the facilities in the areas we visit, nicked across the lane and into *The Crusoe.*

It was a lovely lounge bar, very new and full of leather and brass, great for couples, families having a meal and that kind of thing, a lovely place, but it did not have the same atmosphere, or company, as the *Railway Inn.* So after a swift one it was back across the lane and the increasingly noisy banter of Craig and the local guys.

We eventually decided, after photos being taken of Craig with Maggie, Bill and Alasdair, that it was time to go, so we said our fond goodbyes and headed across the lane to get our next bus, the 2.27pm number 95 to take us to Elie. Alasdair came with us as he was heading home, which was in Anstruther. He comes to Lower Largo each Friday when Bill is staying at his caravan to have a wee afternoon session. Remember, he's in his 90s'. On the bus he asked us if we wanted him to join us for the rest of our trip, but we thought at 90 years old, the dozen or so rounds he already had was enough for the one day. It's probably more than enough for Craig and me, but we're working. That's my excuse anyway.

Craig; The run to Lower Largo was quite pleasant except for John annoying me and I suspect a few other passengers with his singing. It wouldn't have been just as bad if he hadn't been making up his own songs. I made the mistake of helping him find a tune that he could actually hold, and therefore must take some of the blame for the end product. If that wasn't bad enough I'm sure I saw him scribbling down the words so the world has probably not heard the last of his ballad. He'll probably blame me for it anyway.

Lower Largo looked lovely. That was my first bit of alliteration of the day. It really did look great though. We had only just stepped off the bus and we found ourselves in the middle of the best bit of scenery we have wandered through in ages. It must have been good as we spent quarter of an hour charging around photographing everything in sight. That's about 12 minutes more than we usually allot to sightseeing.

The Crusoe Hotel is the larger of the two pubs in the village. It looks really nice and probably quite expensive too. There is an area on the pier which has tables and chairs, is surrounded by a plate glass windbreaker and must have the best view of any pub in Scotland. Actually on a sunny day like today I would say it would beat anything I've ever seen at home or abroad.

189

John; So as the bus pulled up at the stop in Elie, we said goodbye to Alasdair, got off the bus, and wandered up the street to check out the situation of the next bar we planned to visit, *The Station Buffet Bar.* Alasdair had said it was a great wee bar. But first of all we needed to have a walk round the town to let you all know what it is like.

Buffet Bar, at least the Barmaid seems pleased to see us.

Elie is a lovely wee town with a beautiful Harbour. I'm beginning to think that all the wee towns in the East Neuk are like this, and it is no bad thing. They are very nice and picturesque. So when we finished our walk we headed back up the road and into *The Station Buffet Bar.* The name of the bar suggests a waiting room in some station or other, but it is a great wee bar, another worth a visit. The barmaid, Kimberlie was great company and very funny, as were the three local guys. We spent a great 40 minutes or so in their company and enjoyed every minute. We would have liked to stay longer, but we were already behind schedule because of the great time we had in Lower Largo. This was turning into a great trip, lovely towns and great pubs with great barmaids and interesting locals. Craig was starting to wax lyrical about coming to the area for a few days holiday.

Craig; We chose to enter the 'Railway Inn' for our first pint. As soon as we got in the door I knew we had made the right choice. This is exactly the kind of pub we are always looking for. It was bright, cosy and very friendly. Just to make it perfect the drink was reasonably priced. Maggie, the barmaid, was very nice and chatted away to us throughout our visit. We also got talking to two of the best characters we've ever come across on our travels. Bill and Alasdair are quite a double act. Their patter was unbelievable and kept us laughing for ages.

They told us the story about fooling a female tourist who had been pestering them one day. Apparently they told her that one of their favourite games on cold winter nights in 'The Railway Inn' was strip dominoes.

I think John had been only half listening up to this point, but the mention of erotic table games got his attention.

I didn't have the heart to tell him that the old boys were only kidding about their high jinx in deep mid-winter.

Between stories of wild nights in various pubs and the odd joke they've played on unsuspecting tourists we learned that Alasdair actually lived in nearby Anstruther while Bill had a static caravan on the site in Lower Largo. He commutes between the village and his home in Eaglesham, just a few miles from us in East Kilbride. Talk about a small world!

I don't really remember how many drinks we had in the Railway but I will say those old boys can really put it away. We all left at the same time, no doubt to the great relief of Maggie behind the bar.

Barmaid Rating; ����☐☐☐,

Goin' Roon the Edge

Alasdair came with us on the bus as he was going home to Anstruther. He was definitely up for a pub crawl though, but probably thought that he would end up looking after two West Coast drunks. He made the wise choice and stayed on the bus when we got off in Elie.

John; Like most of our trips, they do not go to plan, and this one was to prove no different. We got our planned bus, the 95 I think, to take us to our next port of call, St. Monans. We sat on the left hand side of the bus, the side away from the coast and were only what seemed like five minutes into the journey when we passed the signpost telling us that we were entering Pittenweem. I was mixed up. I thought Pittenweem was after St. Monans, and so it turned out to be. We had run right past St. Monans. The bus skirts around the top of the town and there are no houses on the side of the bus we were on. That was not how Craig put it! I was to blame.

I told Craig this was not a problem. Kate has some distant relatives who, I think, might still live there, if they are alive, and years ago we visited them a couple of times. I assured him it was a lovely town, very similar to Elie with the nice houses and wee harbour. He seemed to think this was all right and we agreed to say no more about it. I bet he slags me to death for this minor mix up.

Craig; While we had been in The Railway Inn, Alasdair had suggested we visit The Station Buffet Bar when we reached Elie. He knew the barmaid in there apparently. I got the impression he knew a lot of barmaids. Anyway he gave me some sweets to give to her and I agreed that I would. But I have to admit I was a bit worried about doing it. There's a name for old men who offer young girls sweeties, and I don't mean 'daddy'. As it turned out I forgot all about them anyway, so I dodged a potential hard slap in the gub.

We had a good time in The Station; proving old Alasdair knows his pubs. The barmaid was a good laugh and joined in on the friendly banter at the bar. Kimberley, the barmaid, told us that the Station had been named Sunday Mail Pub of the Year in 2008, and I could quite believe it. The pub was very modern in décor with huge windows letting in lots of light. We enjoyed the patter of the three other customers and could quite easily have stayed on. But we had places yet to visit, and apparently totally miss, thanks to 'John the Navigator'.

Barmaid Rating; 🍺🍺🍺🍺

St. Monans is quite a large, small town. You would think a bus which stopped there would be the ideal vehicle to get you into that town. Not so, apparently. I still don't know how we missed it, but we did.

Having never laid eyes on the place before I can just about get away with not recognizing it, John, however, had been there before and therefore had no excuse for not clocking the fact that we were hurtling through the town he had been banging on about for weeks.

Pittenweem's best barmaids give it some chat.

John; Pittenweem is another lovely wee town. We walked all round it and agreed that after a day or two we would not be able to distinguish one from another, they are all really nice towns with lovely harbours and friendly locals and barstaff, unlike some of the morons we have met running bars in other parts of Scotland.

After sussing out the place we went into a bar called *Larachmhor Tavern,* at least I think that was its name. At first glance you are not sure if it is a bar. There is a sign beside the door advertising all the things it sells, and near the bottom is the word beer, so in we went. Inside it is a bar, and another great bar. The barmaids, I think their names were Micha and Carrie were a great laugh and we had a great time in their bar.

Craig and I have never had a trip where every bar we went into was as good as today's, and the staff and locals as friendly. The East Neuk is definitely a place well worth a visit. I imagine St. Monans, the place we missed, is just as good.

We found the bus stop and discovered we still had about half an hour till our bus. Our ability to keep to, or even read a timetable was as usual, starting to go out the window. There was a pub across the road from the stop called *The West End Bar,* I think, so in we went. By the way, I apologise to the bar owners after Lower Largo if I have mixed them up or got their names wrong. We had a great time there and my memory is not that great. Anyway, *The West End Bar,* if that was its name was a nice wee pub, and although we only had time for a quick one, we enjoyed it thoroughly.

Although it may seem that Craig and I had put away a vast amount of bevy so far on this trip, (and so we had), this is not the only reason for our trips. The scenery and the people we meet are the other main reasons, and today we fulfilled all these aims, ending up with a wee cargo is just a bonus.

So we wandered, or staggered back across the road and got our bus, another 95, to take us on the 50 minute or so journey to St.

Andrews where we had 20 minutes to wait for our bus back to Glasgow. The journey to St. Andrews passed quickly as I think we both slept all the way. Our brief glimpse of the University town showed it up in a good light-it was still a nice evening, and the town looked very up market. We plan to spend a bit more time there on our next trip which will cover the rest of the East Neuk of Fife.

Craig; Pittenweem is quite a small town but it has always been special to me. The last time I'd been there was about 45 years ago when I was but a lad, in the Boy's Brigade. We were on summer camp and I have never forgotten the place. Mainly because we were made to run up and down the very steep hill in the town for about an hour every morning, before breakfast. That kind of memory stays with you.

While we were wandering round the harbour, I filled John in on the history behind our stop in Lower Largo.

The Crusoe Hotel was named after Robinson Crusoe, a fictional character based on the 'true' story of Lower Largo man Alexander Selkirk. Daniel Defoe liked the story of Selkirk's life on a deserted island so much he changed almost every aspect of the story and produced his famous book Robinson Crusoe. Selkirk was actually marooned on a desert island by the crew of his ship but it was because he was a complete arsehole. He complained, argued and fought with everyone he ever met. They simply got scunnered with him and put him off the boat. Even when he returned to Lower Largo after being rescued he fell out with everybody and was asked to leave. Not exactly the stuff of legend then. Incredibly, it's been said that just after they marooned him on that desert island, the entire crew were lost in a storm. So it would seem that Alexander Selkirk may have been a bad tempered, argumentative bugger, but he was also a lucky one.

By this time John demanded two things from me. The first was that I had to stop talking and the second was that I buy him a drink as quickly as possible. To that end we entered The Larachmhor Tavern.

It has recently been renovated by the look of it. The whole place was very bright and modern. These are two things I don't usually like in my pubs, but I'm willing to make an exception in this case. The Larachmhor is a great wee pub. The staff was very friendly and so were the other customers.

The Barmaids, Micha and Carrie chatted away to us. I think they liked the idea of two old geezers wandering around the country getting blootered. Although I did notice they didn't like it quite enough to buy a book.

A young bloke with an i-phone looked up past issues of The Sun and found the feature they did on us. For a few wonderful moments we were minor celebs, but the moment passed quickly. The pub is owned by the same person who owns the Station in Elie and you can see the resemblance in the décor.

Going back up the hill to our bus stop reminded me of my BB days, especially when I had to stop halfway up to avoid my lungs bursting.

Barmaid Rating; 🍺🍺🍺🍺

John; The X24 left on time, whatever time that was, and the journey back down to Glasgow was spent in quiet slumber. A great way to travel! By the time we got off the bus in Glasgow, we had been over four hours without a drink, nothing to be proud of I hear you say, but it still meant that we had sobered up and our hangovers were beginning to kick in.

As is our normal, we wandered down West Nile Street and into *The Horseshoe* for a quick one. We only had time for one as it was late. For the first time in living memory, or what's left of it, Craig did not finish his pint. He said he was not enjoying it. This was worrying for me as it had never happened before and he's too big to carry home if he collapsed.

A bag of chips from The Blue Lagoon brought him back to life. I think it was the extra vinegar we demanded. We reckon they water it down because your jaws are never clapped together. We sat in the station and ate our chips then boarded the late night train back to EK. Irene picked us up at the station and ran us home. What a woman!

So ended a great trip, one of our best, to take in about half of the East Neuk of Fife. I hope the second part of the Neuk is as good. It's a great place and well worth a visit. And it can be done in one day, a long day, but still a day. What else are you going to do anyway?

Craig; With a little time on our hands we decided to check out The West End Bar.

We had a quiet pint in there, very quiet as a matter of fact. Maybe they keep all the 'fun' people down by the harbour. The bar itself was clean and tidy, just not very lively.

Barmaid Rating; ,

With only 20 minutes in St. Andrews there was no time to look for a likely watering hole so we just shuffled around the bus station till our bus came in.

The trip back down to Glasgow passed in an alcohol fuelled flash. Back in Glasgow we stopped off at our usual halt, The Horseshoe Bar. Either I'm getting old or the beer wasn't so good, I suspect the former, but I had to leave at least half a pint of lager behind when we left for our train home.

John; *My spends for the day; (and it's a lot)*

Bus fares;	£0.00 (God bless the bus pass)
Train Fares;	£0.80 (Train Home)
Food;	£1.70 (chips in Blue Lagoon)
Snacks;	£3.00 (crisps and stuff for bus)
Drink;	£35.00 (only a guess-could be more)
Total;	**£40.50**

I know many of you will think this is a hell of an amount to spend on drink, and it is, but you've got to remember I bought drinks for Bill and Alasdair in Lower Largo. Also remember I got a Plaque from Alasdair for nothing. What a day!

197

Par for the Course

(Up to St. Andrews after passing through Crail,
We drank a few beers and heard the odd tale)

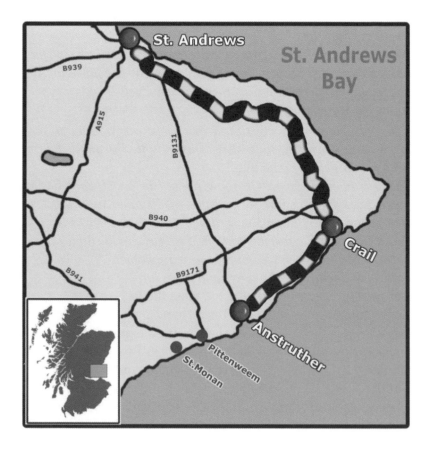

Anstruther-Crail-St. Andrews

Goin' Roon the Edge

John; We only decided to do the Second half of The East Neuk of Fife trip the day before we carried it out. The first part we did on the Friday, we had a chat on the Sunday, and the next day, Monday, we were on our way again. No rest for the wicked, or people who need a book out for the Christmas market.

It was not too difficult for me to work out the bus times as we were acquainted with the area, although we did manage to miss out an entire town, St. Monans, on the first half of our East Neuk experience, although drink was involved.

So after diving around on the Sunday night organizing the timetable and making up pieces, Monday morning found me walking down the wee hill to collect Craig at about 7.40am. It was another miserable day in East Kilbride, but as happened on Friday, the forecast for the East of Scotland was better, and so it turned out.

Recently, I've had nothing bad to report about the behaviour of our drivers, the people we always thank when leaving the bus. Today however, it was back to normal. When Craig and I got on to the main road, about 20 yards from the bus stop, we looked round and saw the No. 18 approaching. It passed us as we were approaching the stop and pulled into the stop to pick up one person who was waiting. I told Craig not to rush and I hurried on. Just as I was lifting my leg to get on, the bastard tried to close the door. Nearly took my leg off. He tried to kid me on by saying he never saw us. Being a nancy boy and coward, I thanked him and we all got on the bus. But I did rant and rave to everybody else. Think I will write a letter of complaint to the bus company, or maybe I won't! When we got to Buchanan Street Bus Station I thanked him on the way off.

Craig; When we started out doing our little trips it was on the understanding that we would do no more than one a month. We set this limit for very good reasons. Given that our first attempt at putting a book together was called 'The Cheap Way Round', the biggest reason seems obvious; we wanted to keep our costs down. Even using our bus passes, a certain amount of money is spent on our days out and about on the highways of Scotland.

Some might say, and I'm thinking of Irene and Kate in particular here, that we spend a hell of a lot of money on our cheap days out, added to that there is the physical side of the equation. Consuming large amounts of beer has an effect on the body, well it does on mine anyway. The day after a particularly strenuous journey can be really tough. But with a whole month to recover, both financially and physically, we have always managed to pull it off.

Now John has upped the stakes considerably. He has demanded back to back trips to the East Neuk with only two days in between. Only time will tell if we survive unscathed.

So it was only three days after we had enjoyed the delights of Lower Largo and Pittenweem that we set off once more for the East Neuk. Personally I was feeling more than a little scathed as we made our way down to Glasgow to start our journey.

As usual the bus was packed with commuters, most of whom were listening to their very noisy music. It occurred to me that the noise level probably went up a few decibels when they actually put their headphones on, my reasoning being their big empty 'heids' must amplify the sound. As you may be able to tell, I was not in a great mood. When John told me about the driver trying to pull away before we could get on, my mood did not improve. Something would have to be done about this man. My first thought was, of course, to write a strongly worded letter of complaint to his employers, but eventually I decided on a more direct form of protest. I'd teach him a lesson he would never forget. As we got off the bus at Buchanan Street I made a point of not thanking the driver. Please do not feel sorry for this man. He had it coming!!!

John; The X26 we boarded was the same one we got on Friday, so it was the same journey with nothing new to see. We spent the time trying to make up humorous titles for each chapter of the book. We have only one double trip to do after this one, so we thought it was time to start working on the various things that need to be done to produce a masterpiece like what this is.

Don't know why I bother, Craig thought all my ideas were crap. I know he will make them up himself. The truth is they will all be much better than anything I could think up.

A well kept hotel - well they kept us out anyway!

As we approached Leven Bus Station, where we could have played safe and changed buses, I said to Craig that we should stay on this bus to Lundin Links and change buses there. Not only would this be unbelievably exciting, but it would give Craig an opportunity to photograph the big local hotel, which is very unusual as well as being a local landmark. The other reason I told him for doing this was that being a big hotel, it would have a big bar where we could sneak a quick one before our next bus arrived. He agreed only because he knew he would be slagged by me if he didn't.

Needless to say it all went slightly belly up. The sun was out, the hotel looked great and Craig got a couple of lovely photographs. The problem started when we tried to get in for our quick one. The bar was shut, and it was my fault.

I told Craig we only had about 20 minutes to wait and this was no big deal. We then asked a local lad if there was a pub near. The nearest one was in Lower Largo, the place we had started our trip last Friday and about a mile walk. Needless to stay we wandered over to the bus stop and waited in the sun for the bus. There was a baker's across the road with a great smell coming out of it. I couldn't resist and ended up going over and getting a cake snowball, you know, the ones with the jam in the middle and coconut flakes all over the outside. It was magic. Craig said he wanted nothing, and that's what he got.

Craig; I was looking forward to a good sleep on the bus to Leven, but I had reckoned without John's enthusiasm. He wanted to work on the book's chapters names. I did the only thing I could think of and just pretended to be asleep. Unfortunately, there was a very gossipy wee wumin sitting two seats away from us.

It wasn't just that she talked constantly, but she had such a high pitched voice it would have made your eyes water, mine did. John was not fooled by my sleeping routine because of this, and he kept going on about those bloody chapter names. At Cumbernauld bus station the problem with John and the screeching woman was solved, but not in a good way. A couple of women got on with the world's noisiest baby. This kid could have been used instead of one of those sirens they have on Fire Engines. It, he or she, didn't stop for breath. John and the screechy woman didn't stand a chance. As far as I know they both stopped talking, it was hard to tell.

Goin' Roon the Edge

The nearer we got to Leven, the more agitated John got. He was speed reading several bus timetables, over and over again. Usually he is quite happy doing this sort of thing but today was different. He was coming across as very nervous, a bit like a lab rat on dissection day.

The thing is he wanted to change our itinerary. That's usually a no no, and for good reason. Any time we change things at the last minute bad things happen, and today was no different.

We had been going to stop in Leven for a quick pint before moving on to Anstruther. John wondered if it might be an idea to stay on our present bus till we got to a place called Lundin Links where we could get off to enjoy a pint in the big hotel of the same name.

I blame myself really, but only a wee bit. Seeing him so confused about what we should do I told him I was OK with whatever he wanted to do. He took this as a green light for his half-baked idea and we got off at his hotel.

It looked very pretty, it looked very big, and, unfortunately, it looked very shut. After spending a good five minutes calling him names I ran out of puff and we walked back to the bus stop we had just left. I was feeling very guilty about some of the names I'd called him, and for some of the adjectives I'd used as well. So I suggested that even if the hotel had been open, it was so posh that they probably wouldn't have let us in anyway.

John was very quiet on the journey to Anstruther, quiet for him anyway. I put this down to embarrassment at making a complete arse of himself with our first stop. But it is equally possible that he was simply planning his revenge. Anyway our bus took us right down to the harbour area. This was very useful as it allowed us to see the layout of the place in terms of where to find the pubs.

John; The bus to take us along the East Neuk to Anstruther arrived dead on time and we enjoyed a lovely run along the coast of Fife to Anstruther. On the way we passed St. Monans and tried to work out how we had gone right past it on Friday. We worked out what we had done wrong, drank too much in Lower Largo!

The bus took us right down to the harbour and off we got in brilliant sunshine. It was blowing a bit of a gale though.

The Ship Inn, Anstruther. Where you'll need a boat load of money if you're paying a visit.

Anstruther is a fairly big place compared to the other villages we had visited in the area and from the size of the harbour and the old photos we saw in the pubs we visited, must have been a big fishing port in the old days.

After wandering about the front for about 15 minutes, quite long for us, we found our first pub right on the front. It was called *The Ship Tavern*, and looked good from the outside and was a lovely pub inside. It was filled with old photographs and memorabilia and had a great atmosphere. The thing that was not so great was the price of drink, we paid well over £7 for a pint of lager and a vodka and soda, and it was skooshy soda at that. What's that all about? Craig nearly choked on his pint. Apart from the prices it was a great wee pub to have one, and only one drink in.

So with the kitty reduced greatly, we wandered along the lovely front filled with ice cream and chip shops. There were dozens of them. It was also lunch break for the local school and hundreds of kids with black and red blazers invaded the front to buy their dinner, chips and curry sauce. The fat kids of the future.

We wandered back up off the front to find cheaper drinking establishments and the first one we found was called *The Smuggler's Inn*. The pub was all right, the prices were better and the barmaid was pleasant enough. But it didn't live up to the image of its name. After a round there we went out and in our quest to find the best pub in Anstruther, went into *The Bank* next door. It was one of the most depressing places I have ever been in. It only struck me later that it had been a bank, and the place was just as depressing as old fashioned banks were. A quick one and we were out.

It was just about time for our next bus so we wandered back down the hill to the harbour and waited for our bus to Crail.

Although I have slagged off the pubs we were in, it is only my thoughts. Anstruther is a lovely place and well worth a visit, and I'm sure the chips and ice cream are great.

The 95 bus turned up on time and we enjoyed the run along to Crail, our next port of call in our visit to The East Neuk of Fife. We got off the bus on the main street, up from the harbour. I think Craig's legs were bothering him as he suggested just walking along the main road till we found a resting place, and you know what he means. The resting place was *The Golf Hotel Crail,* they must put the town name on the pub wall incase you forget where you are.

It was a lovely wee bar and again, very atmospheric. But the barmaid had no interest in making conversation with us. I asked her for the best way down to the harbour, so she knew we were strangers passing through, so we had one drink and passed through.

We walked back along to the turn off for the harbour, which was right opposite a bar. So I asked Craig if he wanted to go down to the harbour, which we should do, or just go right into the pub. You've guessed it, he gave me his camera and I wandered down to the harbour myself and took a few photos. It is a beautiful harbour, as they all seem to be in this area. The East Neuk really is a place worth visiting. I think one of the reasons Craig couldn't be bothered going down to the harbour, apart from his sore legs, was that he took a great photo of a made-up jigsaw of the harbour in the window of a wee shop on the main street. I think he will use it in the book. What a lazy person he is.

On the trail to a great wee pub in Crail.

Coming back up from the harbour, I found Craig in the bar of *The East Neuk Hotel,* and what a great wee bar it was. The reason is the same one I go on about, not the prices or the décor, but the barman or maid and the locals, and they were all great company. The barmaid Isobel was great fun, but she wouldn't let Craig take a photo of her, and she looked great. She must have a secret to hide. We had a great time in the bar and all too soon it was getting to the time when we had to leave for our next bus. So with fond farewells to Isobel and the two locals we were talking to, they wished us all the best in their own way, which I can't print.

Craig; *We had a look round Anstruther harbour and took quite a lot of pictures. There wasn't much going on in that area and we wondered if it was still a working harbour.*

John was convinced that it was no longer a fishing port. I wasn't so sure as I could definitely detect the not so faint whiff of fish. It was so strong that I believed it must be coming from the area in the harbour where they chuck all the fish that they can't sell. The thing is, if I'm wrong about all of that, then there is a very large fish restaurant in Anstruther which would be best avoided.

One or two of the boats in the harbour were very impressive. We particularly liked the sail powered herring drifter which is part of the Maritime Museum based in the town. The guys who worked these boats must have been right hard buggers.

After all this sightseeing we were very thirsty. Luckily there was a good looking pub right next to the boats we had been admiring. What a coincidence I hear you say.

'The Ship Tavern' really looked the part and its location could not be faulted. It even looked great inside. We were still congratulating each other on our good fortune at finding such a great place when we discovered the price of the booze. It was outrageous. We came to the conclusion that we must be subsidizing the maritime museum across the road. The pub had

a large ship's steering wheel sitting in the bar and we wondered if that's what they had bought with the extra beer tariff we were being charged. If so then they've got a long way to go before they can donate another ship to the museum. So there's not much chance of the locals enjoying reasonably priced booze any time soon. We like boats but we don't want to buy one, so we only had one drink and moved on.

Barman Rating; 🍺🍺🍺,

John; Our next bus, another 95 arrived on time, like all the other buses and took us the half hour run into St. Andrews. I had been to St. Andrews to see the Open Championship years ago and had never seen much of the town, so this was a new experience for me. The guys in the last pub had given us a note of three pubs to visit. Two, they said, were great men's pubs, the other would be full of Americans and we would be able to sell our books there no problem.

The first thing we did when we got off the bus was to head down to the Old Course and photograph ourselves in this historic setting. I was surprised that Craig was so interested in doing this as he hates golf and everything associated with it. However, the chance of a great photo shot overcame any aversions he had and we took photos of each other at the edge of the 18th green and then walked down the 18th fairway and Craig photographed me on the wee stone bridge going over the Swilken Burn. An American couple came wandering over to the bridge and were absolutely delighted when Craig offered to take a photograph of the two of them on the bridge. You'd have thought they had just won the lottery. We both enjoyed it as well.

It was starting to rain at this stage and we decided we had had enough of scenic grandeur and history and we wandered up to the 18th hole, round the corner and into a bar called *Golf Place*.

**Does this place suit us to a tee,
or is it a bit rough looking?**

It was a normal type of bar and the prices were normal. We were expecting to get ripped off as it was in a very touristy area, but there you go, not everybody in Scotland is trying to rip off the tourists. One was enough as we had noticed that the bar where all the Americans would be was on the corner. So we finished our drinks in this very pleasant, and reasonable bar and went out, along the road and into the *Dunvegan*.

Craig; I'm not sure why we chose to go into 'The Smugglers' first, it was probably just the name, maybe we thought we sounded more interesting than 'The Bank'. Actually anything would sound better than that. It wasn't a bad wee pub; it just wasn't what I'd been expecting. From the outside it looked like a traditional old Scottish pub. Inside it looked a little bit like a well looked after working man's club.

The staff were fine but seemed happier talking to each other than to us. I don't actually remember how much the beer was, but I think it must have been cheaper than the last place because John wasn't frothing at the mouth when he got his change back. One pint was enough for us and we moved on.

Barmaid Rating; ▮▮▮,

'The Bank', next door looked a bit more up market than its neighbour, and this time the theme was continued on the inside. That was a bit of a pity really, in my opinion. It was obvious the owners had spent a lot of money renovating the place, and quite recently I think. I would have asked but there was no one else in the bar area. Staff seemed to be a bit thin on the ground as well. Since it was lunchtime I would have expected the place to be a lot busier. 'The Bank' has an extensive menu but I only saw two people having a meal in the place. Don't know if that says anything about the food or not. We couldn't afford to eat there even if we wanted to. The décor didn't do much for me either. It was too dark and sanitized for my liking. I would imagine the furnishings probably came from Ikea.

In my opinion 'The Bank' would make a good library or, at a pinch, a bank. They were also playing that mindless musak which annoys me no end.

Barmaid Rating; ▮▮

Apart from the harbour, I would have to say Anstruther was a bit of a letdown for me. I had really been looking forward to it, serves me right.

John; As promised, the place had a good few Yanks in it, but they were all in conversation and it would have been rude to butt in just to get a cheap sale, and as we only had a couple of books with us, it didn't seem worth the embarrassment.

It was a very nice bar and the prices were not too bad considering the setup of the place. The young barman was very friendly and helpful and made us feel very welcome and at home. Pity all bars couldn't train their staff so well. Craig reckoned he was great because he would get great tips from the rich tourists. He might be right, but I think he was just properly trained and well brought up. I gave him a 50p tip out of the kitty when we bought our second drink, just to annoy Craig. We had a nice time in the bar even though we didn't sell any books. Got to relax sometimes.

By this time we had to head back up to the bus station, so we had no time to visit the other two pubs our friends in Crail had told us about. Not to worry, we had a lovely time in St. Andrews. We both reckon that St. Andrews, like other big towns and cities in Scotland will need a day each to do them justice. Sounds like a project for the future.

Craig; Things could only get better, we told each other, when we reached Crail. We were correct, but not straight away.

'The Golf Hotel Crail' was our first stop in the town and it certainly looked the part. Inside it was all Fife Stone and wood panelling with beams on the low ceiling. In fact it was more or less exactly what you would expect to find in a nice wee hotel on the coast of Fife. It was just a pity about the staff, 'soor faced' and 'brusque' would be the adjectives that spring to mind. Maybe it was the Monday morning blues or something. We were certainly not made to feel welcome. Things were looking grim. Compared to our last trip, which was only a few miles from this place, today's little adventure was going fairly badly. So far we hadn't found even one decent bar, and we were fast running out of pubs to visit.

Barmaid Rating; 🍸

John, for some reason I couldn't quite fathom, decided he wanted to do a bit of sightseeing. This was very definitely out of character for a man so dedicated to booze sampling. It must be the sea air.

I had one look at the hill down to the harbour and immediately volunteered to keep him a space at the bar of the 'East Neuk Hotel'.

As soon as I entered the hotel I felt our day was getting no better. The place was empty, completely empty. I was about to

211

go back out the door, to wait for John, I still didn't fancy that hill, when I heard a noise. Away through the back I saw someone moving around and thought it was worth investigating. I'm glad I did.

Through the back of the hotel I found a bar and pool room. I don't particularly like pool, it slows down my beer drinking, but as they say beggars can't be choosers. With our track record so far that day I really couldn't pass up the chance of a decent bar.

There were two blokes playing pool, which is surely not that unusual in a pool room. What is unusual though is that they were singing songs from the 60s' film 'Mary Poppins'. This led to a more general film quiz. It was great fun. The barmaid Isobel joined in and we had a good laugh. After all the nonsense we had put up with earlier, this place was exactly what was needed.

A legend in his own imagination.

Goin' Roon the Edge

John had, by this time, photographed everything of interest in Crail or else he had just got bored. Either way he joined us in the bar and we all had a good time joking and storytelling.
Neither of the pool players or the barmaid wanted their photos taken. We asked if it was for security reasons, social security that is. It's an old joke, but it got us a laugh as we left to continue our journey.

Barman Rating; 🍺🍺🍺🍺

John; The bus, the X24 left on time and we dozed most of the way to Glasgow, where we arrived dead on time.

For some reason, I was feeling great. I think drinking vodka and soda instead of pints is not as alcoholic and you are not as bagged up as you are with pints.

We wandered down to *The Horseshoe,* and because of the times of our EK train, we had to have two rounds, which I really enjoyed. I had two pints of Best, which I think I enjoyed so much because they were the first of the day.

I think it was the 10.18pm train we caught, although I'm not sure, and Irene was at the station to take us home. So ended another great day on the road.

This meant Friday's and today's trip had covered about eight towns in the East Neuk of Fife. This is a great area of Scotland and well worth the visit before our Scottish Parliament do something stupid like stopping the bus pass.

Craig; St. Andrew's is only a few minutes up the road from Crail by bus so we were still in a good mood by the time we left the bus station to find some golf themed drinking dens.
Since we were so close to the famous Old Course, John insisted that we pay it a visit. Personally I could've done without traipsing around looking at large areas of well mown grass. But he was so excited about it that I felt I couldn't really deny him his wee treat. He was like a dug with two tails.

Goin' Roon the Edge

Round at the famous wee bridge whose name escapes me he demanded I take a series of pictures of him in a selection of poses.

The rain had started by this time but he would not be put off. I reckoned that if we spent any more time there we would be eligible to pay green fees. As we were coming away an American couple wandered over. I noticed the same crazy look in the man's eyes as I'd seen in John's, so I offered to take his picture.

The first pub we tried was called 'The Golf Place'. Imagine that in St. Andrew's of all places. It was actually a lot better than we thought it would be. We had been expecting the usual tourist prices but given it is a world famous golfing venue, the prices were fairly reasonable. Either that or we had just got so used to paying over the odds for everything on the East Coast that we had become brainwashed, or conversely, we were just half cut.

Barman Rating; 🍺🍺🍺

Round at the 'Dunvegan' we had our last drink of the day, if you don't count 'The Horseshoe' in Glasgow. It was a very comfortable pub as you would expect in this area of the town. The service was great, very efficient and friendly. My theory is that the staff knows that they are on to a good thing with all those rich American golfer types who like to tip generously. If you've ever been to America you'll know that tipping is a requirement. You will find yourself in a whole lot of trouble if you don't leave a 20% gratuity behind when you leave.

I assume that they continue to tip the bar staff at this level when they come over here. Let's hope it never catches on with the rest of the pubs in Scotland. That would be the end of 'The Cheap Way Round'.

After listening to me going on and possibly on about having to pay the bar staff extra just to do the job they were supposed to be doing in the first place. John had the cheek to leave a tip. I wouldn't have minded so much if it hadn't been for the fact that he took it out of the kitty. Half of that tip was from me!!

Barman Rating; R R R R

The bus back down to Glasgow was so comfortable we fell asleep almost immediately. It might have had something to do with the refreshments we had earlier, who knows?

We only had time for a couple of beers in 'The Horse Shoe' before returning to EK.

Today's trip was very much a game of two halves. The first half was pretty grotty. Firstly we couldn't find an open pub, then when we did they weren't up to much.

Happily along came the second half and things picked up considerably. We found a good friendly pub then enjoyed another two in historic St. Andrew's.

John; *My spends today;*

Bus fares	£0.00 (viva the bus pass)
Train fares to EK	£0.80 (still a good deal)
Trash for bus	£3.50
Pieces	£0.00 (from fridge)
Drink	£33.00 (again a guess)
Total	**£37.30**

I believe oldies like Craig and I spending our hard earned pensions round Scotland is helping the economy. Although I have no idea how the economy works. If that's true, I should get a job along with the other numpties in the Scottish Parliament.

Billeted in Banff

(Two great pubs then into 'The Castle',
What a dump, no worth the hassle)

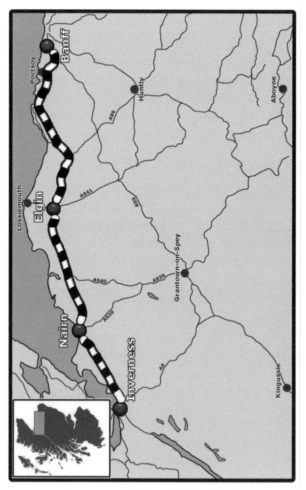

Inverness-Nairn-Elgin-Banff

Goin' Roon the Edge

John; The first of our two day trip away, yes Craig and I were going away for an overnight without the women. The reason for this is that the distance to travel Roon the Edge from Inverness to Aberdeen could not be done in a day. This was the first time we have had an overnight. We were like two schoolboys getting away with something. The planning involved was immense.

Apart from the buses and pubs, we would have to book a room. After studying the maps and organizing where we were going, we decided to stay in Banff. So with the help of Kate's pal Ann, who has a friend who lives in Portsoy, we booked a bed and breakfast in Banff called Gardenia. A good choice.

We decided that since we were going to be in Elgin and Inverness, although not stopping to sample the pubs, we should e-mail the Waterstones in these towns since neither of them had taken any of our two books so far. While we were at it, we decided to e-mail Aberdeen as well, as they are stockists of our books. We felt like real businessmen doing all this pro-active sales stuff, and remember, we're old.

You could have knocked us down with a feather, did the three stores not go and order a total of about 100 books between them. Our excitement was tempered by the realization of the weight involved in humping them about, and guess who would be doing most of the humping. Can't complain though, Craig's a nightmare with his arthritis.

The days before were spent packing books for the different stores and getting all the paperwork done. Because Kate and I do the dispatching of the books, the stock in our house is starting to go down. Craig and Irene are desperate to get rid of some of their boxes, so I've told them we will transfer some boxes up to our house in the fullness of time, or whenever.

Craig; *When we started out on this book we decided that it should begin with a really special journey. On a trip round Scotland starting in England seemed quite special to us. It*

217

seemed only fair that we should come up with something equally special for the final sections of the book. Given that the book is all about day trips around the country, finishing with a two day trip seemed to fill the bill nicely.

Actually it is quite possible to travel to Inverness from Glasgow, then on to Aberdeen and back down to Glasgow, again all in one day, but it would be far from enjoyable. There would be no time for sightseeing, no time to talk to local characters and of course no time for the occasional social drink, so no point in doing that then.

Our original plan was to go to Aberdeen first then make our way across to Inverness. John had spent a lot of time working out the details and was really quite chuffed with himself. It was only after he had produced one of his famous, highly detailed spreadsheets, that he realized it was cobblers. We had to carry 95 books with us to deliver to the three branches of Waterstones across the North East.

The most obvious boob in his masterpiece was a geographical one. On our trip round the edge of Scotland it is rather hard to justify visiting the town of Elgin. Don't get me wrong, Elgin is a very nice little town, it's just that it is not on the edge of the country. But since the bookstore there had ordered 40 books I decided to leave John in the dark, for the moment.

The other problem was that using his first plan for the trip would mean that we would be humping a large, and therefore heavy, pile of books right across the North East. On the first day we would only be getting rid of twenty-five of them in Aberdeen, leaving us with the remaining seventy to trail around the Highlands.

The penny eventually dropped and John realized that we should be doing the trip the other way round. This meant we would get rid of the vast majority of our books within the first couple of hours of arriving in Inverness.

Goin' Roon the Edge

John; I organized the buses, so my first task was to blow £1.00 each and book seats on the Gold buses from Glasgow to Inverness on the Thursday morning and the Aberdeen to Glasgow one on the Friday evening. It's always a relief when the Gold bus is booked. Luxury to the fore. Craig in the meantime was checking out all the pubs we may visit on his magic web.

Even though this was a special trip, I still had to get the pieces and fancies ready for the day. I was hoping Craig had something special for the bus.

The books filled one huge case and one smaller one. Thank God they have invented the cases with the wheels or we both would have ended up in Hairmyres Hospital with hernias. Craig pulled the small one and I took the big one. It was the least I could do.

Because of the problem we were going to have lifting the cases on and off buses, Kate made the magnificent gesture of getting up early on the Thursday morning and running us into Glasgow to catch the Gold Bus to Inverness.

I actually drove. We picked up Craig at 7.30am, which was plenty of time to catch the 8.30am bus; at least I thought it was plenty of time. As soon as we were on the new motorway into Glasgow, the traffic backed. There was no way in my mind that we would make the bus, so I got off the motorway at the Paisley turn off and drove through Pollock, Shawlands and on through the back streets of Glasgow. Hope there's no CCTV cameras on the lights I went through or I'll be jailed. We arrived at the bus station at 8.29am. We drove up the road for buses only and Craig and I dived out of the car, shouted farewell to Kate and rushed, or hobbled quickly through the bus station to stance 51 where the bus was just about to leave, we were exhausted, both mentally and physically.

In typical miserable Scottish fashion, the wee man loading the cases told us we should be at the bus at least 10 minutes before departure but said he would let us on as a favour. I thanked him profusely. If he could read minds he would be away checking to see if his mother was real. The driver told us he was a wee arsehole and not to worry.

Breathless with exhaustion and excitement at catching the bus, we discovered it was very busy and we would have to sit in two isle seats, me behind Craig. As we sat down the gentleman beside Craig said he would switch seats with me so we could sit together. What a real gentleman. If I had had one of our books with us, I would have given it to him to read and really screw up his journey, but our cases were so heavy, we had not brought any extras to give away when I am drunk or sell to unsuspecting pub patrons who had one too many.

Kate had driven round to the car park and came into view as the bus pulled out, so we waved to her, but she did not see us because of the fancy tinted windows on the Gold Bus.

We were on our way north for the adventure of a lifetime, or a night in a Banff bed and breakfast. We were happy anyway.

The run up the A9 is really beautiful. It might be rated one of the most dangerous roads in Scotland, but it is without doubt one of the most scenic roads anywhere. Anyway, the road is safe, it's the drivers who are dangerous, and that's a fact.

It was a lovely, but foggy morning and this led to some amazing views of fog below you in wee valleys. I thought it was great. The fog soon cleared though and the bus bounded up the A9. Craig reckoned there could be a division of German Panzer tanks hidden in the fog. The man's mad, or is he? More on the Germans later. The free tea, scones and tablet followed. They were magic. We were in such a good mood, linked to Craig's Scottish Patriotic fervour, that when we passed a place called Killicrankie, he burst out into an old Scottish song I think the Corries sang called 'The Brae's o' Killicrankie ooooo'. Thank God he only knew the chorus, and that was bad enough, but very patriotic and uplifting.

An interesting thing I noticed was that when we passed a field on the side of a fairly steep hill, the cows were all standing facing up the hill. As Craig is from the country I asked him if this was a normal thing. He had no idea, if you know, answers on a letter etc. etc.

After all this excitement, we settled down to enjoy the rest of the journey. Apart from a wee loud man boring everyone on the bus about the refurbishing of his highland cottage, and Craig moaning about the air conditioning being too cold, the journey passed quickly and soon we were through Aviemore and arriving in our Highland capital, Inverness.

Craig; Getting a lift down to the bus station was the icing on the cake as far as I was concerned. It meant we didn't have to trail the books on and off the number 18 down to Glasgow, but best of all it meant I didn't have to get up too early in the morning. You just can't beat a nice leisurely drive in a comfortable car when the alternative is squashed into an overheated, noisy uncomfortable rattle trap of a bus.

That's the theory anyway, but things don't always work out as 'planned'. Just ask John. We had plenty of time to get to the bus station. It is only about ten miles from East Kilbride to Glasgow city centre, so giving yourself a full hour for the journey might even seem a bit generous. That of course is only if you have forgotten about the rush hour. To cut a long story short, I could have cycled there quicker.

I have to admit that John did a great job getting us there in time for the bus. He also did a marvelous job of scaring the crap out of me. At times I just had to shut my eyes and hope for the best. I was also hoping he wasn't doing the same.

As we got to the bus the wee man who was loading the cases had the cheek to tell us off for being late. If either of us had been able to catch our breath this little nutter would have gotten a mouthful, as it was I had to settle for giving him a particularly derisive stare. I think it did the trick, he won't be doing that again anytime soon.

John; Our first task was to deliver the books to the local Waterstones in Inverness. We knew the address and roughly where it was, but when you leave a bus station, you can never be sure which way you are going, so I stopped and asked a parking meter man. I had our delivery note out and asked him if he knew the directions. Mistakenly, I had out the delivery note for Aberdeen, but when I asked him where it was, he knew immediately it was in Aberdeen and he knew the directions. This was even more amazing as the man was obviously a native German. Could be a bit worrying if Craig is right about the Panzer Tanks hiding in the fog, or I'm off my head.

Being a martyr, I let Craig wait in 'Blackfriers Highland Pub' while I took the big case and wandered off to deliver our first books to Inverness. I was very proud.

After delivering the books, I returned to meet Craig in the pub and still had time for a swift vodka before we headed off to the bus station to catch our first bus on our trip 'Roon the Edge'.

Craig; Up in Inverness we got off the fabulous Gold bus and grabbed our book filled suitcases. I had Googled the Eastgate Centre on my wee smart phone. Not only had I shown John a map of the area but also a picture of the centre itself. However, that was a bit technical for John who stopped understanding technology when the slide rule was phased out in favour of the pocket calculator.

What he needed was to be told by someone in authority exactly where he should be going. Unfortunately he chose a traffic warden, and a foreign one at that. It might have helped if he had remembered he was actually standing on a pavement in Inverness and not wandering along Union Street in Aberdeen.

It is embarrassing enough to have someone mock you in public but when the person making the jokes is a German national, a nation not usually noted for its sense of humour, you know that you really have made a complete arse of yourself.

After getting precise directions to the Waterstones store, which incidentally were exactly the same as the ones I'd given him, John was happy to let me sit in the pub while he delivered the books on his own. Personally I think he wanted rid of me as I was having a great laugh at his expense.

The nearest pub was 'Blackfriers Highland Pub' and it was only as I crossed the road to it that I remembered that I was supposed to give the landlord a copy of our last book. The owner Del had featured in that book and had actually bought a copy of our first one. It's a bit ironic really that we were trailing a large number of said books around with us but we couldn't spare one to give away.

Jack's Bar & Bistro. We only had wee bit
of a wait to get served.

I chatted away with Del and his wife while I waited for John to finish his deliveries. For some reason it took him exactly as long as it took me to finish a pint of lager. He only had time for a quick half. As I didn't want him drinking alone I joined him.

Barmaid Rating; 🍺🍺🍺🍺

John; The number 306 took us along the coast and dropped us off in the wee bus station in Nairn, our first port of call. It was a glorious day and we had a walk down to the harbour, which was alright, but not as picturesque as some we have seen on previous East Coast trips. Nairn is a nice place, in a quiet sort of way, but Craig was starting to get edgy. There was no sign of a pub at the harbour and it was a good walk back up to the main street. Peace returned when we came upon our first pub called 'Jack's Bar and Bistro'. The name Bistro obviously put Craig's back up. You don't get Bistros in Auchinleck, but when we got inside, it was a lovely wee bar and we felt at home right away.

Allison serves up the pints in Uncle Bob's Bar.

Goin' Roon the Edge

We enjoyed a couple of drinks and the Barmaid was very nice and even told us of a good pub to visit up on the main street, so after saying our goodbyes, we wandered through the town, which is very nice and worth a visit, and found the unusually named 'Uncle Bob's Bar'. We had to go up a big flight of stairs to find the bar, humping the remainder of the books, but it was well worth the effort. It is a great wee bar, and the barmaid Allison was great. She told us the history of the name of the pub. Unbelievably, her uncle Bob owned the bar and was famous for naming places. Shouldn't have laughed as she then told us that her uncle Bob had just died at the early age of 65, same as me. I hate hearing things like this. Thankfully Allison was over it and was great company. We were just finishing our drinks when a woman came into the bar pushing a bike. It turns out she now owns the bar. I asked her how she managed to get the bike up all the stairs. She told us she lives in the flat upstairs and had just bumped the bike down the stairs. I offered her a fiver if she would try to cycle down the stairs. Drink was starting to kick in. She was also very nice and we enjoyed our time in Bob's before we had to leave. This is definitely a bar worth visiting when you're next in Nairn.

Craig; On the short journey to Nairn we scoffed a few sandwiches, for medicinal purposes, and enjoyed the wonderful scenery. Actually it is just as well that scenery was well up to scratch because Nairn, in particular the harbour area, is quite a bit less than fantastic. I suppose it is functional as a harbour. That is to say that people who want to get on or off their boats can do it there, but if they want to appreciate an idyllic, traditional Scottish harbour they will have to up anchor and find another port. This place is dismal, and that is on a sunny day. I usually like a nice harbour scene to photograph but in Nairn I didn't even take my camera out of my bag.

What was required to cheer us up was a good drink, so that's what we went in search of. 'Jack's Bar and Bistro' didn't look like it was about to supply that but, as they say, appearances can be deceptive.

As a rule I don't usually go into Bistro's. To be honest it's more the kind of people who do go into Bistro's who keep me out of the places. But let's face it, we were desperate, so in we went.

It was actually a lot better that I imagined it was going to be. I am happy to say that there were no pretentious half-wits hanging around in this Bistro, other that John and me, of course.

Apart from the lack of posers, the bar also had only a few arty-farty artifacts, and that's not easy to say. In fact it was quite an ordinary little bar. The only really weird thing about the place was the cobbled area around the actual bar. What is that all about? Uneven floor surfaces are bad news at the best of times, but in a pub they are positively dangerous. Even sitting on my bar stool was a bit of a roller coaster ride, and not to be recommended. Apart from that I enjoyed our short time there. The barmaid was quite friendly and the beer was pretty good too.

Barmaid Rating; ☒ ☒ ☒ ☒

We thought that since it was unlikely that we would be back up in Nairn for quite some time, if ever, we really should visit more than one of the town's boozers. So it was out into the sunshine once more, in search of another good pub, and within five minutes we found one.

'Uncle Bob's Bar' doesn't sound like a particularly great man's pub, but it was. Unfortunately the pub was up a huge flight of stairs. Even on a good day, in the medical sense, those stairs would have been a bit off putting, but when you're carrying a half hundredweight of books around with you it's a real killer.

Allison the barmaid was very nice and chatted away to us the whole time we were in the place. She was not too keen on getting her picture taken, but I can be very persuasive when I put my mind to it. In this instance I simply employed a bit of blackmail. I told her we would talk about her if she didn't. We enjoyed our stay so much we bought another drink even though there was only another fifteen minutes before our bus was due. It was about this point that I realised something was wrong with my stomach. I was in agony. At first I put it down to drinking very cold beer, very quickly. Later on I began to think it was perhaps carrying the case up all of those stairs which was causing me the problem. I manfully decided not to tell John. Not because he would be worried about my health, but rather, he would be panicking in case we had to turn back and he would miss out on all the unrestricted drinking he had planned. I therefore kept my complaining to a minimum and simply harped on about those bloody stairs. What was required here was a good escalator.

Barmaid Rating; 🍺🍺🍺🍺🍺

John; The 50 minute journey to Elgin, on our next bus, the number 11 was again very enjoyable. The countryside is very nice, but flatter and not as dramatic as the West of Scotland.

Craig, always on the lookout for any minor slip ups on my part, casually mentioned that he had just noticed a sign for Lossiemouth, about 10 miles away, on the coast. I had always imagined Elgin was on the coast. It's not. Craig was enjoying himself at this major screw up. But is it? Does it really matter if the towns we visit 'Roon the Edge' are actually on it. At the end of the day you do your best, so I just told Craig to get a life.

At the end of the day, Craig couldn't give a shit where he is as long as the pubs are open. A bit like me then.

Our first task again was to deliver our precious cargo, the books. Fortunately, the shopping centre Waterstones was in was attached to the bus station so we had no difficulty finding it. Books delivered, we headed out to discover Elgin. Because of my foul up in that Elgin is not on the coast bit, we did not have to wander down the traditional hill to the harbour, so we concentrated on the main street.

Elgin is just a bigger version of the other wee towns almost everywhere in Scotland. Almost all of the shops can be found in any high street. I am not saying this is necessarily a bad thing, it's just how things are today. It's the specialty wee shops which crop up which make towns different, and Elgin has quite a few of them. It's a nice town and again well worth a visit.

"Whit dae ye mean there's nae beach in Elgin?"

We visited two pubs in Elgin, the first was called 'Iconic'. I felt that this was an unusual name for a pub, and it attracted us into it, not because we were gasping for a pint. Inside it was nice and the customers and barman were friendly without wanting to make conversation with us. We had a couple there mind you, said our goodbyes and walked along the main street for a while.

A sign for a pub up a wee lane attracted our attention. We like pubs up wee lanes. This one was called 'Flannigans', and we shouldn't have bothered with the effort of going up the lane. It was a dreich place and lacked any sort of atmosphere. The barman made no attempt at conversation, so we had a quick one and departed.

Craig; In Elgin I was still feeling pretty bad so I decided to torture John a wee bit. I thought it would take my mind off my troubles. After we delivered the books I suggested that we should maybe take a wee stroll down to the harbour to take a look at the fishing boats. He was less than amused that I was having a go at him and his inability to read a map. Suffice to say there followed a period of dark muttering until we both found something else to annoy us.

Our first stop, 'The Iconic', wasn't really so annoying, it was just an ordinary pub and that was fine. I think we were expecting something special. If you're going to call your pub 'The Iconic', it might be an idea to make an effort in tarting the place up a bit.

Barmaid Rating; 🅁🅁🅁

The second pub we checked out was called 'Flannigan's'. As soon as I saw the sign I thought 'not another fake Irish pub'. After visiting it I thought 'what a pity it wasn't a fake Irish pub'.

Bland and soulless would be an apt description of the place. That's not what John and I called it, but we're trying to cut down on the bad language.

Barman Rating; 🅁

John; The bus run along the coast to Banff took about an hour and a half and the bus detoured through many towns that I had visited when I was on holiday in the area many years ago. All of the towns we went through looked lovely and most had great harbours. The towns I remember going through are Portgordon, Buckie, which is a big place with a great harbour with a shipbuilding yard and everything, Portessie, Findochty, Portnockie, Cullen, which looked to have a great Golf Course and lovely railway viaduct. We then passed the top of Sandend beach before going through Portsoy, where I spent a holiday one summer not long after Kate and I were married. I was much younger then. The bus passed where out holiday hotel should have been, but it wasn't. It had been replaced by flats. Ah well what can you do?

John digs an impressive escape tunnel out of Flannigan's.

Amazingly, one thing I remember on that holiday many years ago is that one night we were in the bar and I was playing the puggy, and I won the jackpot. It was £5, which was a lot of money then and I was delighted. In my excitement I shouted 'drinks all round'. I think I had seen somebody say that on the telly. The bar was packed and the round was over the £5 I had just won. In my defence, I'd probably had a few by then.

Before dropping us off in Banff the bus went through one more wee town, Whitehills, which also looked great. It was getting dark when we got off the bus and it took us a while wandering about before we found our digs, the 'Gardenia'. We were made very welcome by a lovely couple, I think they were English. Our rooms were great and after dumping our stuff and filling in our breakfast wish list we wandered out into the darkness to hit the town.

Craig; Back on the bus again I was much more comfortable as the pain in my stomach had subsided. Unfortunately it was soon to be replaced by a different kind of pain altogether. John was on a wee trip down memory lane and I had to listen to it.

Apparently, as a boy, he had holidayed in this area quite often. He was really getting into it, talking about all the little towns he had visited back in the distant past. I asked him if all those Viking raids weren't a wee bit scary for him, but he didn't even notice my cheek. By this time I was getting a bit nostalgic for the sore stomach I'd had earlier as it was more interesting than listening to the schoolboy delights on offer in 1950s Portsoy

To make matters worse our bus driver seemed intent on visiting every village and hamlet along this stretch of the North East coast. The bus eventually stopped in Castle Street in Banff and we got off. We wandered up to the top of the street and then down to the other end before realizing that the bus had let us off directly across the road from our digs, 'The Gardenia Guest House'.

We were very impressed with our digs and I suppose at some time John will take all the credit for finding them. It was actually either a friend or relation, or maybe even a friend of a relation who suggested this house as a good place to stay, and whoever they are, they were right.

Goin' Roon the Edge

It was all high ceilings, wood panelling and furniture that actually looked as if it belonged there.

The couple who run 'Gardenia' were very nice and couldn't do enough for us. There were two rooms for us. One was right next to the dining room by the front door and the other was somewhere up the rather grand staircase. Moving faster than I had all day, I pounced on the downstairs room. One look at those stairs and with the memory of the ones down in Nairn was enough to make up my mind as to where I would be resting my head that night.

John; Banff is a fairly big place compared to some of the places we came through and we spent a fair bit of time wandering about looking for somewhere to eat. There were plenty of carry out places, but the only place for eating in looked a bit too up market for us, so we found a pub and wandered in to consider our next move.

'Barclay's Pub' is the name of the place, and a great pub it is. The barman and his son were great company, and we were shown some amazing card tricks, which were brilliant. A couple of locals, Ainsley and Ally were great company also. Ainsley owns another pub in the town called 'The Railway'. She said she came down to this pub for a change of drink, and scenery. We had a great time in the pub, and following their instructions, found a curry house we could sit in. We enjoyed our curries, which filled a space.

We wandered up the hill, (there's lots of steep hills in Banff), along a road, passed a lovely looking building which is the local hospital and found 'The Railway Inn'. This is another great pub and the barmaid, Ainsley's daughter Kayleigh was great company. She said she had been in the pub business since she was eight, and was definitely well trained.

We enjoyed our time there before I made the mistake of listening to Craig who wanted to finish the night by visiting another pub we had passed near the hotel. This dump was called 'The Castle'. Don't go there unless you are a Jakie who has no taste in music. We had a quick one and left.

Banff is a great wee place and so were the pubs, or as Meat Loaf would say, ''Two Out of Three Ain't Bad''.

It was bed time and we wandered the few yards to our Hotel. We both had no real idea of how to set our mobile phone alarms, and we needed to because we were up at 6.30am to catch our 'school bus'. So we decided that if one of our alarms worked, that person would phone the other. Craig phoned me. I've no idea if mine would have worked, who cares, home tonight.

That was the end of our first of two days on the road, it was very enjoyable, and the books we delivered might even cover the cost of the day's bevy.

This is a really nice part of Scotland, and one worth a visit. The thing we both noticed most is how friendly and open the people who live there are.

Craig; We were travelling light so it only took us a few minutes to stow our gear and re-assemble at the front door ready for a night on the town. Putting it that way makes it sound quite exciting but for the first half hour it was anything but. We couldn't find a pub and even finding our way down to the seafront proved quite difficult.

Eventually we did catch sight of the sea, at least we think it was the sea. It was very dark by this time and we thought we could see lights shining on the water. To be honest it could have been a very large puddle we were looking at. By that time we were past caring and in great need of alcoholic refreshment. Finding a good pub was now a priority.

Almost by accident we happened on 'Barclay's Pub', as it turned out it was a very happy accident. As soon as we entered we knew we were on to a winner. The guy at the bar, who turned out to be the owner, spoke to us straight away. He asked us if we were on holiday and if we were enjoying ourselves. He introduced himself and then the barman, his son, and the four other customers. They all seemed like friends rather than customers actually. It was really great to be included in the company from the moment we came into the pub.

The owner, apart from being a bit of a patter merchant, turned out to be a really good close magician. His card tricks were amazing. He had cards appearing inside sealed bottles and even inside an apple. We were like a couple of small kids at the circus. This guy could load a deck of cards with aces if he wanted to. I'm surprised he's not a millionaire, or in jail. Actually he told me his pub had been up for sale for ages but there had been no takers. Like most pubs nowadays, his bar was not attracting enough punters to keep it viable.

Barman Rating; 🍺🍺🍺🍺🍺,

One of his customers owned a bar at the far end of Castle Street so we decided to pay it a visit.

Before that, however we needed to get something to eat. This should really have been easy enough to organize but either Banff is very deficient in sit down eating places, or they are all located in a part of the town we never came across. There were of course plenty of take away joints, but we were a bit wary of them.

The curry house was the only place we could find but it looked really good. I would have preferred it if the place had been a bit busier as this would show that locals liked the food in there. Maybe Thursday nights are a slow night everywhere in Banff.

Perhaps it wasn't the cleverest idea for someone with a 'Jippy Tummy' to be eating a curry, but there was little other choice. Anyway it was really tasty, especially when washed down by a great pint of Cobra lager. After a great meal it was time to get back down to business.

Curry House Rating, A Hot 🍺🍺🍺🍺🍺,

'The Railway Bar' turned out to be a really nice little pub. Much of this, I think, was due to the young barmaid who was in

charge while we were in. She was very friendly and, of course, very efficient. The bar was really quite busy and you've got to hope this means that the 'The Railway Bar' has a bright and long future ahead of it.

Barmaid Rating; ⧮⧮⧮⧮⧮,

Sometimes even the best of us gets things wrong. The thing is we had struck it lucky with everything so far in Banff and I thought we could do no wrong. Turns out we could!

'The Castle Bar' is just a few steps along the road from our guest house which to my mind made it ideal. Who wants to have to walk for miles after finishing your last pint of an evening?

The trouble was 'The Castle Bar' was pish. It was full of weans, Jakies and what appeared to be a group of trainee prostitutes. To make matters worse it seemed this little group of misfits gets to choose the music which is played at an ear-splitting level in the bar. I think I'm being charitable when I say 'played' as it didn't seem to have a tune attached. To replicate the effect of their chosen music, I would suggest putting your head inside a large oil drum and letting several Jakies hit it with baseball bats.

Barman Rating; ⧮

We managed to avoid bleeding ears long enough to swallow our beer, then we called it a night.

On our first ever two day trip the first day had gone really well apart from the agonizing stomach pain obviously.

Hotel Rating; ⧮⧮⧮⧮⧮,

John; *Spends for the day*

Bus fares;	£0.00
Food;	£15.00 (Curry and a pint)
Drink;	£40.00??
Total;	**£55.00**

Many of you will be thinking, how can anybody spend that much on drink? Well I can, so there!

Doin' time in Peterhead

*(Go to the Broch an you'll think you're in heaven
Because some of the boozers are open at seven)*

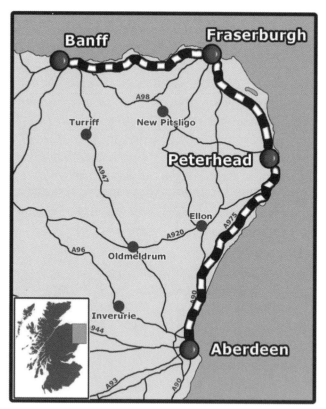

Banff-Fraserburgh-Peterhead-Aberdeen

Goin' Roon the Edge

John; If, for any reason you are reading the book backward, we were staying overnight in Banff last night as part of a two day trip in the North East of Scotland.

Refreshed and full up after our full Scottish Breakfast, mind you it might have been an English one as the lovely couple who owned the hotel are English. Anyway, I don't know the difference although it might be something to do with black pudding and totty scones, we wandered down the very steep hill to get our special bus, the 7.35am number 271 to take us to Fraserburgh.

When I was arranging our buses for the trip, which is a great skill by the way, all the buses from Banff to Peterhead took between two and a half and three and a half hours, except the 7.35am bus which took just 50 minutes. We didn't really want to be up this early, but the difference in times gave us little choice. I was worried I had read the timetable wrongly, this is happening a lot recently, so the first thing I did when we talked to our first locals in Banff, was to ask what was the score with the early, quick, bus. It is the morning school bus to take the kids directly to the academy in Fraserburgh. The guy I was talking to looked at the two of us and said, 'Don't worry, perverts are allowed on the bus', this was the far north of Scotland after all.

I was a bit concerned because Craig and I were on a bus once which stopped to collect children at the local Glendaruel Primary School and the driver, Donald, a very nice man, asked us to get to the back of the bus. It made us feel like a couple of old perverts. There was no problem this time, the kids were more like grown-ups. This also made me feel very old, but not a pervert.

Craig had a concern that we would be arriving in Fraserburgh at about 8.30am, and what were we going to do till the pubs opened. I assured him that Fraserburgh was one of the largest fishing ports in Britain and all the pubs would be open at

237

7.00am so the fisherman could have a pint after their shift at sea. I sounded more confident than I actually was; you've got to put on a front after all.

I'm sure Craig wasn't feeling very great as he suggested he wouldn't mind a cup of tea. This is the first time Craig has mentioned tea since the day I met him. Something was wrong, but he assured me he was ok and it was only the early hour that was the problem. I wasn't so sure.

Craig; *Part one of our last trip around the edge of Scotland had gone really well, with only a couple of exceptions. Before the second part began I was looking forward to a good night's sleep. There was a big day ahead of us and I wanted to be at my best. Considering John's plan meant we had to be on the bus at 7.35am, we were going to need all the sleep we could get.*

It was unfortunate then that I developed an irritating cough soon after I got into bed. After an hour or so of trying, and failing to get off to sleep I gave up and spent the rest of the night sitting up in a large and fairly comfortable armchair. I probably nodded off several times but only for a few minutes at a time. As you could imagine I wasn't feeling at my best by the time my phone alarm went off.

Next door in the dining room John was being annoyingly cheerful to such an extent that I was seriously thinking about loosening the top of the salt dish. I'm a dangerous man to annoy in the morning.

For reasons I cannot explain I decided to have the full Scottish breakfast. It seems incredible that anyone, who only the day before, had suffered agonizing stomach pains, then drank more than a few pints of lager, and topped off the evening with an Indian curry, would think it sensible to have a large greasy fry up first thing in the morning. It actually sounds like a drawn out Scottish suicide attempt.

We said our farewells at the guest house and walked down the hill to the bus stop. One of us strode along the road, whistling tunelessly, while the other stumbled along like one of the living dead. As they say every picture tells a story.

We really had to get this bus as it was the only one that day to take the direct route to Fraserburgh. It took about 50 minutes to travel the twenty or so miles. If we had missed this bus it would really have wasted our trip entirely. All the buses, and there aren't that many, which run between Banff and Fraserburgh go via Aberdeen. That's a journey of well over 80 miles. It's also insane.

A sight for sore eyes, especially when your stomach's a bit iffy.

John; After we got off the bus, making sure Craig didn't punch any of the children goodbye, we found our way to the harbour. For anybody who has never been to Fraserburgh, the harbour itself is worth the visit. The fishing boats are huge, they looked great. It is not an attractive harbour, but men like me who like ships will love it. As we were standing about taking a few photos, and trying to look tough, like fishermen, I noticed a wee café in amongst all the sheds that hold the fish and stuff.

Angela and Pearl want to sign up for the trip.

It was called 'Angela's Tearoom'. In we went looking nothing like fishermen and the place was just as I hoped it would be. It was fantastic, long wooden tables with plastic covers and a great smell of frying filling the place. I loved it. The owner, Angela clocked us right away and asked us what we were doing in a wee Tea Room in among fishing boats, but in a nice way. When we told her what we were doing, Angela and her pal told us they wanted to join us on our trips. They were great company and made us really welcome. The local guys were great company, even if the older men's accents were very difficult for me to follow.

Although we had had a full breakfast not much more than an hour ago, we felt we had to order something, so I had a coffee and a roll and sausage, I think Craig had the same with tea. We thought we were doing alright in the food front when a guy came in and ordered 'a Bacon Cheeseburger with a couple of Sausages on top'. What a man. Made us feel like wimps, which we are.

We had a great time and Angela gave us her e-mail address so we could keep in touch and let her know when our next book is out. We promised her she would be in it, and she is. So feeling as full as a wulk, we wandered out into the Fraserburgh sunshine.

Craig; When we got off the bus John was congratulating himself on an incredible piece of timetable planning while I was congratulating myself on being able to hold on to my full Scottish breakfast.

John finds a boat he might be able to handle.

Actually I think the whole thing was a set up. It's a well-known fact that John's favourite fantasy is to get an early morning drink in a pub. This was his big chance. Fraserburgh, being a fishing port, has pubs which open for the convenience of the hardy trawler men. He had heard that some of these pubs open at seven in the morning; I could swear he was salivating when he told me about this.

We were standing in the street trying to decide which direction to take when a van driver came over to help us. He thought we must be lost, and to be honest I think John always looks a bit lost so it's no surprise when total strangers insist on helping us.

He pointed us in the direction of 'The Royal Hotel' which he said was the only one open at that time. It was really good of him to take the time to help so we felt obliged to try it out.

About 30 yards from its front door we found a good reason to give The Royal Hotel' a wide berth. One of its patrons was standing at the front door spitting large globules of phlem into the street. Neither of us fancied wading through this mess so we passed by on the other side of the street.

Down at the harbour common sense prevailed and instead of a large cold beer we settled for a big warm cup of tea. 'Angela's' tearoom was a life saver as far as I was concerned, although I did lose the place slightly and ordered a roll on square sliced sausage as well. Not exactly guaranteed to settle the stomach of the slightly out of sorts traveller.

Angela and Pearl, who seemed to divide their time equally between working and laughing, made us feel very welcome. John had been worried we wouldn't be allowed into the café because the only time we ever handle fish is when we nip into the Viking chip shop down in Largs. But everything was fine and we enjoyed our visit.

It was while we were in the café that I first heard people referring to this area as 'The Broch'. I didn't know what they were on about but, being a bit of an expert in pretending to be smarter than I really am, I just nodded wisely and kept my mouth shut. The only problem is that I still don't know if they were talking about Fraserburgh or the whole of that bit of the coast. No doubt John will tell me, even if he doesn't know either.

Teamaid Rating ▦▦▦▦▦,

John; Following Angela's advice, we wandered across the road and into 'The Ship'. This is a really great, traditional man's bar, and the barmaid Heather was brilliant and great company. We had a few, I think, and the patter was brilliant. Just as we were thinking we must leave, or we'll be here all day, the owner Mark came and introduced himself to us. What a great guy he is. He showed us all round the various parts of the bar, lounge bar, function room and a bar upstairs with a fabulous view over the harbour. He has spent thousands on the place and Fraserburgh is lucky to have as great a facility in the town as 'The Ship'.

Heather and Mark had filled us in with details of other pubs to visit in the town before we left, but as usual, because we had spent so much time in 'The Ship' and had such a great time, we decided that we just had time for maybe two more pubs.

'The Balaclava' was just along the front a bit so we walked along and went in. To be honest, there is nothing wrong with the bar, but I think it was after the fun we had had in 'The Ship', the next bar was always going to struggle to make an impression. But we enjoyed our pint before leaving to head for our last port of call.

We walked up to the main street and into 'Cheers'. Craig had found it on the web and had said it seemed a good place, and he was right. It is owned by a guy called Dennis, who is Mark's twin brother, although I didn't think he looked like Mark.

This is another fantastic and very unusual bar. Like his twin brother, Dennis has spent a fortune on this unique facility. You go up a lane and the entrance to the bar is on the left. The bar itself is very nice and there is a restaurant in it as well, but it is the outside bit that is fantastic and unique. There is a huge covered area with leather couches and chairs, heaters, big screen televisions that get brighter when the sun shines, a bar, pool table and toilets. The whole place is fantastically finished and spotless. For smokers, and more importantly families, or just people who want to be outside, but still have all the facilities of an inside bar, this place is by far the best I have ever seen.

Local fishermen parked outside the Ship Inn waiting for opening time.

I hope Dennis and Mark get the backing of the locals as well as tourists to have the success their bars deserve.

Fraserburgh is a big fishing port, but it is a great place and well worth a visit.

As time was moving very quickly, it always does when you're enjoying yourselves, we found the bus station and waited in the bright sunshine for our bus, the 269 to take us to our next port of call.

Craig; Our first pub of the day was 'The Ship', and an inspired choice it was. 'The Ship' is what we would call a traditional man's pub. It was great. Heather the barmaid told us that the owner had spent a fortune on renovating the adjoining lounge bar, 'The Galleon', but had decided not to touch the bar in 'The Ship'. He said the locals wouldn't stand for it. Having enjoyed our stay there as much as we did, I can see what he means.

Being from the West of Scotland we rather stood out a bit as soon as we starting talking. Heather couldn't resist asking us what football teams we supported. She said that people up there in the North East just didn't get all this sectarianism nonsense. We all agreed that it was a bit silly in this day and age to define people by which football team they support. It was at this point that Heather admitted that her husband is a real blue nose and even named their house 'Ibrox'. John nearly fell off his stool laughing.

The owner of the pub, Mark, came in and almost straight away started chatting away to us. We had a great time talking about a range of subjects and pubs in particular. Apparently Mark and his family own quite a few pubs in the Fraserburgh area, so if anyone knows about the trade, he does.

He told us that despite having great facilities next door in the lounge, 'The Ship' was still the most popular bar in the place. Even the younger crowd liked to start off their evening in the old bar before moving to the trendier places.

Barmaid Rating 🍺🍺🍺🍺🍺,

Heather had suggested we try a pint in the 'Balaclava' which was just up the road. She said a friend of hers worked there and was always good for a laugh.

I think it must have been her pal's day off. The 'Balaclava' was ok but that was about it. The pub itself was a lot more modern than 'The Ship' and very much brighter. These are features not necessarily on the top of my list of things which make a decent boozer. It also had those booth seats which are best suited to cafes and diners. I hate them. We didn't stay long.

Barmaid Rating ♟♟♟,

Small entrance to a really big pub.

We cut our losses and headed for 'Cheers Café Bar and Tavern'. This is a well named pub. From the outside it is impossible to tell just how big this place is. I actually thought it might be a basement bar but, as we walked up the close, it opened up into an enormous area.

Unsurprisingly, we made straight for the bar, where I immediately had to eat my words about hating modern and bright pubs. This bar was both of these things and all the better for it. A lot of money had been spent on the pub and we appreciated it.

Dennis the owner, and twin brother of Mark down at 'The Ship', came over to us and introduced himself. We chatted away for a while before he took us on a tour of the outside drinking area. It was a real eye opener. I've never seen anything quite like it. The outside sitting area is better equipped than most pubs I've ever been in. Dennis told us that it had won an award for having the best facilities for smokers in Scotland.

Overall 'Cheers' has been put forward for three national awards for quality and service. If you ever find yourself in the North East, I would highly recommend a visit to Fraserburgh, or 'The Broch', and to 'Cheers' in particular.

Barman Rating 🍺🍺🍺🍺🍺

John; Peterhead is, I think, the biggest fishing port in Scotland, but is probably better known for the prison. Around the time of our trip, the prison was celebrating the 25th anniversary of the famous riot when the prisoners took a couple of warders hostage on the roof. They then started throwing the tiles off the roof at the people below. If my memory serves me right, and it seldom does, I think Margeret Thatcher sent in the SAS with instructions to kill all the prisoners. Fortunately, the SAS are not as bad bastards as Mrs. Thatcher and they got the warders released and peace restored without killing anyone, I think.

Craig told me a great story of someone interviewing a prisoner afterwards and asking him how conditions were in the prison. He supposedly replied, 'you can't complain, you get three square meals a day and a good roof under your feet'. It's a great story anyway.

Dennis in Fraserburgh had given us a list of decent men's pubs to visit, but before enjoying ourselves in the local bars, we walked down, it's always down, to the harbour to see the boats. Peterhead harbour seems massive, and some of the ships there are also massive, I've no idea what they all do, but they look fantastic. It's not a pretty place, but I loved it.

Our first pub was called 'Harbour Lights'. It's on a corner near the harbour and it is a great man's pub, just the kind Craig and I love. It was busy and the patter in the place was magic, even though it was hard to pick up the accent.

A guy who looked as hard as nails, and he would be, came over to the bar and asked the barman for Dominoes and the board. Craig, for some reason, thought he asked for a bottle of Bordeaux, he turned to me and said, 'they surely don't sell Bordeaux in here. Senility is creeping up on Craig.

Again, the people we came into contact with were all very open and friendly. When I asked in the bar where our next bar, 'The Caley' was, a guy insisted in taking me outside and showing me exactly where to go, and that's happened to me before, but never in a good way.

We wandered along the main street for a bit to take in the sights, again. It's not a bad place at all. The bar we were looking for, 'The Caley' was proving hard to find. With the instructions I had received from the man in the last bar, I was sure we would have no trouble finding it.

The reason for our trouble finding it was that firstly it didn't look like a bar from the outside, and it had no name on it, but we still found it. When we walked in at first we wished we hadn't. It was a real dump. There were about half a dozen crazy looking guys at the bar and they were all drinking cans. This is unusual and usually not a good sign. But we were in and you can't just turn round and run out. Well I could, but Craig's from Auchinleck. It turned out to be a great wee bar. Everyone was friendly and the place had a great atmosphere. Just shows you, you can't judge a pub before you've had a pint.

We had a chat with one of the locals and he wasn't crazy, so there you are. All the Peterhead crazies must be in the nick.

Craig; The bus to Peterhead followed the usual pattern for buses in this region, it visited every bus stop in every small village anywhere near the main bus route. I don't think a single person got on or off the bus in any of these wee places. Anyway, as I've said before, if these people in these places really needed to travel by bus they should shuffle the 50 odd yards from their houses out to the main road. This would not only cut travel time in half but it would significantly reduce my blood pressure.

As the bus was travelling along what we imagine is the main street in Peterhead we scanned each side of the road to find a likely looking pub. This proved to be more than a little depressing as we didn't find a single one.

Eventually, down a side street, we found what we were looking for, 'The Harbour Lights'. This place looked like a real working man's pub. Everything in the place was basic and functional, not one penny had been spent on decoration. Not in the last 20 years anyway. I had long since stopped drinking beer as my stomach was objecting to the stuff. Now both John and me were drinking vodka, and in 25ml measures at that. I'm pretty sure the pub's other customers had noticed.

This was a pretty tough bar and I was a bit worried they might turn against these two southern vodka drinking softies. But we needn't have worried. All the guys sitting behind us were far too busy threatening each other to be bothered with us. I'm fairly certain it was all good natured banter but it was hard to be sure since I couldn't understand a word they were saying.

The only trouble we had in 'The Harbour Lights' was with a possibly psychopathic dog which, every few minutes, took it into its head to charge around the bar area, crashing into furniture and at least one vodka drinking bus pass traveller.

Barman Rating ♟♟♟♟

We had been given directions to our next pub, 'The Caley'. More accurately, John had been given directions and to be honest I had cause to wonder if he had heard them properly. The reason being that his directions led us back up to the main street where we both had seen no sign of any pubs.

Just as we were about to give up on the search, I spied two of those metal ash tray things which are usually bolted to the walls outside pubs. We had a quick look in the front door and discovered a dimly lit bar inside.

I have often heard people describe Peterhead as a very bleak place but I had always thought they were talking about the weather or even the architecture. It would appear that they might have been talking about the town's pubs.

'The Caley' looked as if all of the colour had been drained out of it. Everything looked grey or beige. The bare floorboards added to the austere look of the place. Maybe the bareness of the place was an embarrassment to the pubs owners. That might explain why there is no pub name displayed outside the place. This certainly stops the pub from filling up with too many pesky tourists. We restricted ourselves to a single drink then made our way back to the bus station.

Barman Ratings ♟♟♟,

John; The journey to Aberdeen seemed to take ages for me. Craig slept most of the way. I was looking forward to delivering our last lot of books to Waterstones and more importantly, getting to a toilet. So before delivering our books, we went into 'The Bridge Bar' for a pee and a pint. This is a very up market bar for the local businessmen. The barmen have shirts and ties on and are very efficient. That aside, it is a good bar and we enjoyed our pints, and I enjoyed the lavy.

We found the Waterstones and made our last delivery. It was a great load off our arms, although we still had the big empty case to haul around.

We still had over an hour till our bus so we headed along Union Street and around a few corners till we found a great wee pub we were in last year and featured it in Still Goin'. It's called 'The Spirit Level' and it's still goin' strong.

The last time we were in the barmaid Susan was brilliant and very friendly and we hoped we would see her again. There were two girls behind the bar and I thought one of them was Susan. Craig told me I was daft and that Susan was younger than the girl I thought was Susan.

We went up to the bar, ordered our drinks and started talking to the barmaids. As soon as we told them what we did, they knew us immediately. The one I thought was Susan is her mother Jackie, I didn't know if I've just insulted Susan, but Jackie seemed happy. Jackie and the other barmaid Julie were great company and we had a great time there. Craig took their photograph, I think, and I'm sure he'll put it in this book.

Craig; We had books to deliver in Aberdeen and remembering the last time we had to do this I was less than happy. The shop we were going to was on Union Street. Unfortunately coming from the bus station there are several hundred stairs to be negotiated on the way up to the shop. That last time I barely made it.

It occurred to me that if our bus went along Union Street we could get off and save ourselves from those dammed stairs. As soon as we had delivered the books John demanded to be taken to the nearest pub as he was suffering from an excess of liquids.

'The Bridge Bar' was quite busy; in fact it reminded me of the 'Horseshoe' bar in Glasgow, but on a smaller scale. It is one of those city centre pubs that attract office workers on their way home from work.

The bar was too noisy for my liking but John's greatest concern had not been to find the best bar in Aberdeen, just one which had a toilet. We had a quick vodka. You can't really use the facilities of a pub without buying something, can you? Then we left to search for a more enjoyable place to have our final drink of our two day epic trek across the North East.

Barman Rating 🍺🍺🍺

John suggested going back to one of our old favourites, 'The Spirit Level', as a fitting place to end our trip. The only problem was he didn't seem to know where it was. He headed off in the opposite direction of the pub and I had to haul him back. As we walked along the road it occurred to me that I had let him do all the planning for this trip without asking too many questions about his competence in map reading.

Not realizing that it's a 10 mile walk to the nearest beach from Elgin should have had the bells ringing but I managed to ignore this lapse in basic geographic knowledge. But not being able to find a pub you have visited several times in recent years is really a big worry. Fortunately I have never had any difficulty finding public houses and I saved the day by steering John in the right direction.

Round at 'The Spirit Level' we got talking to the barmaids Jackie and Julie. It was great to be ending our journeys for this year in a good pub and in good company. I suggested we should have a photograph of the two girls as we had put a photograph of Jackie's daughter Susan in our last book. This caused a bit of excitement with Jackie running off to the area at the back of the pub. To be honest I thought that I had somehow affronted her until I realized that she was off doing up her hair.

Goin' Roon the Edge

It seems our book has been quite well received up in Aberdeen, well with the staff of 'The Spirit Level' at any rate.

Just as we were about to leave for the bus station, Jackie bought us a drink as a thank you for visiting them again. This kind of thing doesn't happen very often, in fact it came as such a surprise John was left speechless for a couple of seconds.

Barmaid Rating 🍺🍺🍺🍺🍺,

Jackie and Julie keep things running smoothly in The Spirit Level.

John; Time was racing past and it was soon time to say goodbye to the girls. We wandered over to the bus station. The sun was still shining, and we went into the station to buy a sandwich for the bus. Although you get a sandwich on this Gold bus, it is a wee thing and as we had not eaten since our two breakfasts, we were feeling hungry, at least I was. I still didn't think Craig was feeling very well. My feelings were confirmed later when he announced that he wanted to go straight home when we arrived in Glasgow, at 8.45pm!!

We joined the queue for the Gold Bus and Craig kept an eye open for the queue jumpers. The queue was very orderly and soon we were settled into our luxury seats for our journey back down to Glasgow.

The sun was setting as we left Aberdeen, on this, our last trip of this book. Nostalgia was creeping in as we left the city and I was moved to write a song;

When I was a lad, a tiny we lad
My mother said to me
When you're old, you'll get a bus pass
And go up to Aberdeen free

At this point Craig had to admit he was not feeling at all well and told me to shut it. I did.

The run back down to Glasgow passed without incident. It was a glorious night and the sun was setting all the way down to about Perth, when it got dark.

We arrived back in the Buchanan Street Bus Station on time and we walked slowly down Renfield Street to the Central Station to catch our train, the very early 9.18pm. It was sad that Craig was not up to our usual visit to the 'Horshoe Bar' on this, our final trip. As the old movie title stated, 'A Bar too Far', or something like that. Craig was feeling terrible, but had not complained all day. I would have.

When I texted Kate to tell her our time of arrival back in East Kilbride, she said she would pick us up at Hairmyres. This would still allow her to be home by 9.30pm for Strictly Come Dancing, or some programme like that.

So ended our last trip of this book, 'Goin' Roon the Edge.

Craig; The journey down from Aberdeen was an absolute nightmare for me, and not just because John had decided to

254

entertain me by singing one of his nonsense songs, over, and over again. I had been feeling pretty bad all day but it all came to a head while I sat on the bus. For an hour I was pretty much out of it before recovering. Strangely enough this coincided with John's sleep pattern.

Despite not feeling too great for a large part of this two part journey, I really enjoyed the experience. On more than one occasion we both had to admit that we were very impressed by the people we met in the North East. Almost everyone we came into contact with was friendly and helpful. The pubs, for the most part, were very good and the buses did what was required of them, they turned up on time. For those among us who like a bit of scenery with their holidays, the North East is a fantastic place to visit.

John; *Days Spends*

Bus Fares;	£0.00
Train Fares;	£0.80 (back to EK)
Food;	£5.00 (roll on sausage and sanys for bus)
Drink;	£40.00
Total;	**£45.80**

Travelling round Scotland and spreading our pension must be a godsend to the economy, at least that's my excuse for drinking myself into senility.

Books by the same authors

The Cheap Way Round.

This first book by the bus pass using pair sees them set out on the road around Scotland. Their mission is to find the best and worst examples of the country's tourist hospitality.The second part of that mission is to do it all on the cheap. No easy task when you realise just how dedicated they are to the art of beer sampling.

Priced £7.99

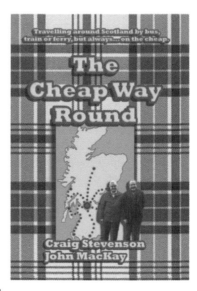

Still Goin'.

The second book in the series sees the much travelled bus pass duo go further afield in their quest to find the best and worst pubs in Scotland. From Inverness in the north to Newton Stewart in the south they travel the highways and bye-ways of this great country trying out beers and bar service along the way.

Priced £7.99